expressed

Hölderlin

Friedrich Hölderlin, 1770–1843

Hölderlin: The Poetics of Being

Adrian Del Caro

 Wayne State University Press   Detroit

95   94   93   92   91   5   4   3   2   1

Library of Congress Cataloging-in-Publication Data

Del Caro, Adrian, 1952–
    Hölderlin, the poetics of being / Adrian Del Caro.
        p.   cm.
    Includes bibliographical references and index.
    ISBN 0-8143-2321-9 (alk. paper)
    1. Hölderlin, Friedrich, 1770–1843—Criticism and interpretation.
    I. Title.
    PT2359.H2D38   1991
    831'.6—dc20   90-25927

Chapter 10, "Shipping Out: Columbus and the Voyage of Discovery," appeared in different
form in *Colloquia Germanica* 21. 2/3 (1988): 144–58.

Book design by Joanne Elkin Kinney

Alla famiglia Del Caro e al nostro caro
amico Enrico Collosetti

Contents

Preface

This *Hölderlin* deals mainly with the poetry and is intended as an introduction to the poet. Part 1 specifies and discusses aspects of the poet's vocation, while part 2 attempts to situate major poems of the late period within the theoretical framework of the question of being.

The reader should refer to existing translations of Hölderlin's poetry as a companion to this work. Among these translations I have found those of Hamburger, Sieburth, and Middleton to be of great assistance for purposes of clarification and comparison, but all translations from the German are my own. With regard to my translations, the following guidelines are in use. Insofar as I rarely offer a "total interpretation" of a poem but, instead treat a variety of texts according to themes established by the poet, the reader should not expect a polished, stylized translation; for this, one should consult the translations cited above. My energy was devoted to providing a rather literal translation and supplementing it with commentary. In so doing, I tried to remain faithful to the text and context and to avoid the superimposing of argument into the texts.

The possible advantage of my approach is a fresh reading and reconsideration of most of Hölderlin's later poetry, since a monograph on the poetry, devoted to the major categories of the poet's thought, moves with greater freedom than is generally allowed the translator who is restricted to a few remarks concerning each poem. For the most part I have relied on the texts as they are given by Friedrich Beissner in the authoritative Stuttgart edition, and, as anyone working with Hölderlin will readily admit, Beissner's work is a source of invaluable assistance.

I wish to thank the Council on Research of Louisiana State University for their support.

Introduction

To attempt to present any cogent picture of Hölderlin's poetry is to look deeper into the nature of poetry than is generally called for by the various modes of discourse. Often a poem, anyone's poem, is subjected to interpretation; the critic operates under the premise that a poem is a riddle merely waiting to be guessed, or a secret code known only to the poet that will now unfold by virtue of the critic's application of special tools. While the reader has every right to expect that poetry has *meaning,* that it is indeed meaningful, still it is difficult when confronted by the best poetry to reduce things to "meaning." "What does the poet mean?" is always a fair question, but, in the case of Hölderlin, "What *is* the poet?" might give us a more generous perspective from which to understand not only the individual's poems but poetry as such.

Insofar as Hölderlin reflected much on poetry, and the question of the possibility of poetry is central to his work, the meaning of these poems is not easily divorced from the meaning of poetry per se. There are many levels on which poetry is meaningful, and Hölderlin had a lot to say on this score without being pedantic, without prescribing for others, poets or readers, how poetry should conduct itself or how others should conduct themselves with regard to it. If it were possible to give a generally satisfactory interpretation of each Hölderlin poem, such that the boundaries of interpretation yielded *this* turf to Hölderlin and *that* turf to another, still one could not identify a separate realm of influence in which Hölderlin was instrumental; for this poet viewed poetry as an analogue to being, and the continuum of being is constantly overlapping, now reaching into the past, assimilating, now projecting into the future while grounded in the present.

Hölderlin was not alone in ascribing great potential to poetry and in recognizing it as a timely factor in the evolution of the human spirit. The years of his mature writings, roughly 1796–1803, saw the blossoming of early German romanticism through the writings of Novalis, Schelling, Friedrich and August Schlegel, Tieck and others. Building on the eighteenth century contributions of Rousseau, Herder, and Goethe, this generation of thinkers held enormous faith in "the word," in the medium of language, and never tired of exploring the connection between what Germans call *Dichtung* (creative writing) and the search for a level or atmosphere of culture that might suggest in the present that cultural unity that moderns have ascribed to the ancient Greeks. But unlike the proponents of romanticism who came to be known as the Jena school, Hölderlin's explorations were conducted, for the most part, on his own. And while we can say that Novalis's view of the novel and his romantic view of the world through or as the novel (German *Roman*) was influenced to a greater or lesser degree by the presence of Goethe, we cannot say the same concerning Hölderlin's late contributions, since neither Schiller nor Goethe has much to do with the direction taken by him in the practice of the poet's vocation.

Hölderlin himself contributed to the idea that Schiller had been instrumental in his career, but it warrants closer scrutiny. According to Harold Bloom, Hölderlin suffered from an "anxiety of influence" in his relation to Schiller, claiming, for example, that he could never break out of his dependence, while in reality the very statement of his dependence on Schiller was a gesture of independence. Writing about Hölderlin's self-effacing letters to Schiller, Bloom describes

> an exercise in self-misprision, because in it a very strong poet evasively relies upon a rhetoric of pathos to portray himself as being weak. The revisionary ratio here employed against Schiller is what I call *kenosis* or repetition and discontinuity. Appearing to empty himself of his poetic godhood, Hölderlin actually undoes and isolates Schiller, who is made to ebb more drastically than the ephebe ebbs, and who falls hard where Hölderlin falls soft. This *kenosis* dares the profoundest evasion of naming as the death of art what is the life of Hölderlin's art, the ambivalent and agonistic clearing-away of Schiller's poetry in order to open up a poetic space for Hölderlin's own achievement.[1]

I think Bloom's analysis of the Hölderlin-Schiller relationship very much captures the spirit of poetry as Hölderlin practiced it, with its suggestion of the agon and the clearing away, the making of space that is of vital importance to Hölderlin.

One of the interesting biographical details that emerges in the case of Hölderlin's productive lifetime is the absence of what we today call a "steady job." After his theological training, Hölderlin made numerous efforts to support himself as a private tutor, often relying on friends and acquaintances to secure these positions, which usually lasted a short while and left him wandering about from one city to the next.[2] Unlike many of his mentors and peers, Hölderlin never enjoyed the economic and emotional security connected with a university position or a position in government. It is interesting to speculate about what might have happened if Hölderlin had found an academic career, some administrative work in government, or a pastorship. The fact we have to work with, however, is that his aspiration to become a poet only grew stronger as his failures in the "business" world accumulated. The growing determination to be a poet is a decisive factor in Hölderlin's poetry, and *determination* is meant here not only as the human act of volition but the ontic event of one coming into one's own.

The Germans have a term for one who writes occasionally, on the side, and it is *Gelegenheitsdichter*. Though in his productive lifetime Hölderlin published less than his peers, a fact which is underscored also by his lapse into madness around 1806, he was anything but a dilettante; in fact, the intensity of his late writing displays a noncompromising tenacity of poetic mission that is difficult to rival. Comparisons are frequently made between him and others, and, while they may be helpful in specific cases, Hölderlin's reliance on poetry and poetry's debt to Hölderlin are truly one of a kind.

The generation whose most creative minds set to work in the 1790s was acutely aware of the transitional nature of German culture. Hölderlin and his peers looked forward with charged anticipation to the role German thinkers might play in the unfolding events of Europe after the Revolution. The so-called golden age of German culture, encompassing the efforts of the classicists in Weimar and the romanticists in Jena, acted as a focus on Germany, placed it in the limelight, and Hölderlin was ready to take up the challenge by establishing a context in which to regard the outpourings of theoretical writings and poetry. The Enlightenment and the Revolution spawned by it were a momentous occurrence of theory followed by practice, and, even if, historically speaking, the Revolution is said to have failed in its ideals, there can be no denying that Hölderlin's generation believed in the possibility of theory becoming practice. Poised as it was on the threshold of the modern age, with its emerging democracies, the generation of the 1790s urgently felt a responsibility to the future. At this time, as Charles Taylor has aptly observed, the artist rose to a prominence hitherto unknown to Europe.[3] Hölderlin's specific effort in the determination of the direction of modern man had to do with the relationship of poetry to being. To perceive that a new age was in the making was merely a first step, but, given that beckoning factor, that challenge, just where did man stand in his relation to past and future? Hölderlin's efforts to find a place for poetry in the here and now hinged on this question.

The poet's interest in the remote past, in this case ancient Greece, is not *preconditions of all culture*

nostalgic, nor is it academic. Hölderlin may indeed have longed to be among the ancient heroes, but I dare say he longed more urgently to be among heroes in the present. And though he shared with academics an interest in learning from and about the past, here, too, he went beyond the norm and addressed the issue of ancient culture's preconditions as the preconditions of all culture, all community per se. This poet's motivations in going back to the ancients were more in the nature of approaching what he called "the source" than they were expressions of *Weltschmerz,* or longing for the fabled golden age. In their writings the ancients dealt with the question of being on manifold levels, with conceptions of nature, gods, and demigods that modern man has abandoned. Just as the poet meant more to the ancient community than he could possibly mean to today's, so too poetry had a greater, more immediate role in the lives of ancients. What man is, in the most universal sense, and what is a community of man in the collective sense, are issues entrusted to the ancient poets, or at least, they were issues which Hölderlin discussed within the ongoing context of determining what man is. Hölderlin, his peers, and prominent earlier Europeans such as Vico, Rousseau, and Herder all "assert the priority of poetry over prose," according to Paul de Man, a priority that links poetic language to the archaic and prose to the modern. The problem with regard to our study of Hölderlin, therefore, will not reside in demonstrating that poetry was a preferred medium; rather, as de Man continues, it will lie in allowing the unique, singular contribution of Hölderlin to emerge, for the present has a tendency to become "single-minded and uniform" on this issue, whereas each thinker, from Herder to Hölderlin, has a separate agenda.[4]

Since Hölderlin was not only a scholar of Greek language and culture but also a poet whose use of German can safely be called Hölderlinian, it is helpful when considering his poetry to recall the priority of poetic language over prose, whether or not this priority is shared by us. Comparisons are indeed helpful for this approach, and perhaps two will suffice for introductory purposes. Goethe, for example, was among many things a scholar of the ancients, and he is justifiably regarded as a classicist in terms of literary history. His best poetry exhibits a balance, a very carefully executed "measure" in spite of the profundity that might attach to the subject at hand, as seen perhaps in his poem "Nature and Art" (*Natur und Kunst*). One is impressed with Goethe's clarity, and one admires the masterful proportions of form and content. Indeed, Goethe's poetry is so successful on this particular score that it seems almost to be a style of prose that has been taught to sing, for the modern reader does appear to sympathize more with lucidity, on the interpretative level, and the advantage of prose should be that its first striving is for lucidity. Now in Hölderlin, on the other hand, we must experiment with our conceptions of what is lucid, what is profound, what is balanced, and we must also exercise greater caution. Hölderlin's striving to clarify is anything but paternalistic, often because the issues he treats are not regarded as instances, paradigms, or lessons so much as I think he regarded the poem as a probe. When the writer is conducting a probe, or a sounding, he is not aware in advance of what he might discover. Consequently, if the poet is in pursuit of something he intuits, and if each poetic event contributes to a greater clarification of what is, what stands between him and all others (including himself and all others), then each poem will reflect a new attempt and its language is tailored to suit. And in the plainest terms, spoken without theory, Hölderlin does not appear lucid. This appearance, however, while it is able to stand in comparative terms, is deceiving, since it is by now well known that some of the greatest philosophical minds of our century see the lucidity of Hölderlin's writing precisely because he dispenses with the established conception of what is lucid in favor of breaching the lock.

In her recent book on Hölderlin and Novalis, Alice Kuzniar points to an important dimension of the poet's style. "Hölderlin interrupts, complicates, and even at times suspends articulated language. He discovers a speech that maintains silence. Paradoxically then, displacement serves to orient Hölderlin's poetic voice; it renders his verse unique and distinct.[5] This observation is in keeping with my view that Hölderlin makes a new attempt with each poem, and Kuzniar also understands that Hölderlin could not have sanctioned the idea of an "organic whole" to each poem, since he constantly revised his work, and withdrew from potentially presumptuous utterances (170). But in spite of any aversion Hölderlin may have had concerning the limitations of language, and in spite of Hölderlin's suspending of articulated language, the fact remains that he *did* write, and that we do have a text. The critic cannot afford to be coy where Hölderlin himself was bold, even if the poet wished not to err by way of boldness. The success of Hölderlin's poetry is a result of his circumspection with regard to language; we read his poetry because he was a great poet, not because he suggested that he or anyone else *might* be a great poet.

Schiller is another poet often compared to Hölderlin, and justifiably, since not only were Hölderlin, Schiller, and Goethe contemporaries, but the latter also endeavored, for a time, to further Hölderlin's poetic aspirations. Again, "comparison" here does not mean the two are alike and is used primarily to shed light on Hölderlin's poetic language. Though Schiller was capable of poetry on occasion rivaling that of Goethe, for him often poetry was an ersatz for prose, and the reader is not struck by any sense of necessity, urgency, searching, while Schiller's didactic and moralizing bent is richly in evidence. One does not immediately know, and perhaps may never truly know, why Hölderlin wrote as he did—with tortured syntax, ambiguous antecedents and

modifiers, and deliberate fragmentation—and yet, the authenticity of his po-
etic language is not questioned, the difficult journey is worth the effort, and,
instead of having been led by the hand or swept off one's feet by some
masterful stroke, the reader of Hölderlin finds clarification by virtue of having
had to work for it. Paul de Man asks a good question with regard to poetry that
might help to suggest why Hölderlin became so important to our century:
"Can we find out something about the nature of modernity by relating it to
lyric poetry that we could not find out in dealing with novels or plays?"[6]
Indeed, let us expand on this; Heidegger wrote neither novels or plays, and
certainly he believed the question can be answered affirmatively even if it
were to include philosophy.

When a thinker in his appropriate medium crosses the boundaries that
critics establish for a particular medium, one finds a lot of speculation con-
cerning the thinker's authority. Nothing invites second-guessing more than the
crossing into another's realm, and yet, man among all creatures is the one who
wanders. For Hölderlin there was no separation of poetry from truth and,
therefore, no essential difference between poetry and philosophy. Novalis,
Friedrich Schlegel, and others called for the reuniting of these artificially
divorced spheres; Hölderlin did a lot less "calling for" and devoted himself to
the task. And in Hölderlin's case the union of poetry and philosophy was not
so much an issue, or a plank within a theoretical platform, as it was the given
with which he worked. In his milestone book on Hölderlin and Pindar, M. B.
Benn discusses how critics often grant Hölderlin legitimacy as a poet, but not
as a philosopher.

> We have become suspicious of all attempts to judge poetry by its philosophi-
> cal content, mistrustful, even, of any marked interest in the ideas of poetry.
> We like to quote the saying of Mallarmé to the effect that "la poèsie se fait
> avec des mots." We are inclined to suspect that those who look for truth in
> poetry must lack the feeling for beauty. We are afraid the preoccupation
> with ideas may kill the appreciation of aesthetic values, and we are doubtful
> whether the ideas of poetry are worth anything anyhow.[7]

Indeed, professional philosophers are generally in agreement concerning who
is or is not a philosopher, though of course even the philosophers have their
preference, but a good part of the problem stated by Benn is that poetry, by its
nature, is less easily canonized. If philosophers are individuals whose work
brings them into contact with the broadest possible implications of what is
true, we might expect that at least many philosophers, following the model of
Plato, break the staff over the poet as one who simply prefers fiction to truth.
This perception, furthermore, is not often challenged by the poets themselves,
as the best poets consider the question to be academic, while among the lesser
poets the question is moot.

Hölderlin clearly has made a name for himself as a poet who is read and studied by philosophers, among others, and today it is impossible to divorce his writings from the philosophical context of the generation of the 1790s in Germany. But the obstacle to viewing poetry as anything but an aesthetic diversion remains, in part, due to the efforts of one of history's greatest "poetic" philosophers, namely Friedrich Nietzsche. For Nietzsche as a young man had a genuine, intuitive love for the writings of Hölderlin, only to abandon his interest in the poet when it became time to set forth the duties of the philosopher, which Nietzsche held to be incompatible with the effects of poetry. Ironically, in the early years of Nietzsche's worldwide reception he was considered by many critics and philosophers to be "merely" a gifted poet, a great literary talent, while his philosophical writings were suspect.[8] Nietzsche's admiration for Hölderlin allowed him to perceive of the poet as mere poet, an unfortunate turn in the life of a philosopher who had so much to say concerning issues addressed by Hölderlin, and in his later development Nietzsche frequently regarded himself as the "mere fool, mere poet" whose writings did not carry philosophical authority.[9] Clearly, Nietzsche was acutely aware of the problem of truth next to poetry, even the great poetic-philosophical work *Thus Spoke Zarathustra* is a testimony to the difficulty of keeping these spheres separated; but what Nietzsche in his better moments was able to see, and appreciate, is the fact that *Zarathustra* is a great work of philosophy because Nietzsche the poet let himself be.

Unlike Nietzsche, and later on Hugo von Hofmannsthal, much influenced by Nietzsche, Hölderlin did not have to contend with an unrelenting ambivalence toward poetry. Instead, Hölderlin became sovereign within the sphere of poetry in the manner of one who knows what he is about, and comes into his own. Though Hölderlin on occasion raised the question of poetry's place in modern society, he did not despair and eventually condemn the poet; indeed, he remained philosophical about poetry, he persevered, demonstrating that it was a real vocation. One who fulfills his calling to such a high degree, and against formidable odds, is not a weakling who succumbs, as Nietzsche would have it, but a rare, affirmative will. What Nietzsche was generally able to praise in himself, namely the overcoming of poor health, a false career choice (academics), a heavy reliance on Richard Wagner and his worldview, he was not able to recognize in Hölderlin, who had to wrestle with demons in his own right. But even if they viewed poetry from opposite sides, still there can be no denying that Hölderlin and Nietzsche had more in common than the fact that both lost their sanity.

Both were individuals of great will and great faith, though it is not so easily seen how "faith" manifests itself here. Nietzsche's cultural criticism, and his scathing criticism of the modern man, were not undertaken in a spirit of hatred but in a spirit of love for humanity. Even the overman, or *precisely* the overman is a measure of Nietzsche's faith in man to become someone greater, to evolve spiritually as he evolves physically. Hölderlin, too, made the condition of man a central issue of his thought, but not by attempting to isolate man in the universe and grounding all meaning in a new man. Both Nietzsche and Hölderlin were enthusiastic about the idea of a natural man, only for Hölderlin this natural man does not divorce himself from his gods, he does not deny his spiritual needs. Hölderlin spoke of man's future as something near, something for which all the components were already in place, while Nietzsche's projection of the overman into a nameless, distant future where the present man's inhibitions are overcome clearly shows him as the cultural pessimist.

Erich Heller has written that Hölderlin and Nietzsche "are possessed by a more intense and genuine feeling for man's spiritual need than is shown by much orthodox belief."[10] Since both thinkers were well schooled in the Bible and in the classics, one is tempted to regard their faith as a vestige of the old faith somehow transferred into a pagan worldview. But the classics and the Bible are threads of a common source, so that whether we speak of gods or God, the real concern is for man. In pagan times the poet and the priest were not separate individuals, as Novalis tirelessly explained in his philosophical writings, and the philosopher, as Nietzsche repeatedly noted, did not have a monopoly on truth and morality before the time of Socrates. Schlegel's call for a new mythology, Novalis's call for the union of poet and priest, Nietzsche's insistence that the proper study of the philosopher is the life of man—all of these expressions of post-Kantian philosophy have the determination of man at their basis. Hölderlin distinguished himself within this context as well, and in his case, for the most part, poetry was the medium of expression as opposed to theoretical prose. In other words, though various individuals since the Enlightenment have written persuasively in prose on the unique capacity of poetry to say something meaningful about being, Hölderlin's use of the medium of poetry placed him within the source moderns generally objectify. And it is not simply a matter of Hölderlin's "use" of poetry for the communication of his special theory of poetry that is at stake here, for Hölderlin's poetry does not represent theory but practice.

Theorists and critics are justifiably in awe of the genuine poet and, as a result, often attempt to draw the poet into their domain, appropriate him, as it were. The genuine poet is one whose poetry is not merely interesting, autobiographical, idiosyncratic, clever, or glib. There are of course countless examples of poetry that are essentially individual, in the sense that the reader or listener is introduced to some individual who speaks in his particular way concerning whatever concerns him. If this were to suffice to describe Hölderlin as poet, surely very few essays and books would have been written about him. The "individual" is a commonplace in modern society, as long as

we do not apply strict ontological categories to the term *individualism*, be-
cause the individual is a product of fragmentation, lack of planning, and
absence of will. Too much poetry is a product of individuals trying to make
their debut known to others; they are fascinated with themselves, perhaps
others will be fascinated, too. It is an old problem.

In one of his greatest philosophical works Friedrich Schiller voiced his
concern for the fragmentary nature of the modern individual. As a species we
have of course advanced, but Schiller was concerned about what has hap-
pened in the meantime to individuals. Why, he asked, did the individual
Greek of ancient times qualify as a representative of his age, while the modern
individual dare not? Schiller answers the question by claiming that "all-
unifying nature" gave its forms to the ancients, while moderns are instead
informed by "all-separating reason."[11] This criticism of the modern individual
was prevalent among classicists and romanticists; indeed, Rousseau had given
the eighteenth century its ideal of nature. Nietzsche took up the problem of
individual versus natural, or collective art, in *The Birth of Tragedy;* the
Greeks could not tolerate the individual on the tragic stage, for individuals are
comic rather than tragic, and Nietzsche argued that the Greeks regarded the
individual in much the same way that Plato regarded the idol as opposed to the
idea.[12] Particularly, German theory is full of expressions detailing the authen-
ticity of the natural, the collective, the universal, as opposed to the rational,
individual, idiosyncratic. It is therefore not surprising to find Nietzsche, in his
later career, speaking of the poet as a mere fool, a mere comic and a magician.
But once again it must be observed that Hölderlin was a poet who triumphed
over the difficulties of the modern individual, and though he was no less
aware of the loss of nature than were Schiller and Nietzsche, in his case the
reconciliation with nature occurs in practice.

In lines that are frequently quoted by today's poets Hölderlin asked: where-
fore poets in paltry times? The wide-ranging implications of the poet's words
could easily seduce us into thinking that the major concern here is a criticism
of the age, but Hölderlin's poetry reveals that poets simply do not have it easy,
not at any time. It is not too much to say that, for Hölderlin, the poets make
time by determining man's place in time. There are, of course, poets who
prefer to be passengers of their age, commentators and bards of the mundane,
individuals hurled about by the same forces that propel all others like so many
passive objects, but whose laurels as poets rest upon the ability to snatch
colorful moments from the general confusion and send them whirling on the
wind like falling leaves. Hölderlin's faith in poetry and in all others, for whom
poetry is, could not allow him to play the role of harlequin, nor was there any
salon great enough to imprison him. It is ironic, though by no means unusual,
that a poet whose great concern is for the proper place of man could find very

bout —

...tle room within his own age. Hölderlin, who attempted to reveal man's situation in the present by recollecting the past and indicating the future, was himself, socially speaking, on the fringe. But speaking now in the language of poetry, it was not he who was on the fringe, but the contemporaries who circumscribed the boundaries of their age too narrowly, too superficially.

The title of this study readily identifies it as a methodology influenced by the writings of Martin Heidegger. Some are prone to take issue with this approach, as Heidegger's philosophizing on being has exerted a wide and, some would say, all-too-wide influence since the 1930s. New methods of criticism, often indebted to Heidegger, have since come into vogue, and some would like to see these contemporary approaches applied to Hölderlin. It is my view that Hölderlin's poetry, which so strongly reflects his faith in poetry, is very difficult to read even for the scholar of German; for this reason, my introduction to a broad selection of the major poems intends to make the poet accessible, readable, with the hope that readers will pursue Hölderlin on their own. Since much of the post-structuralist criticism questions the scholar's and reader's abilities to extract meaning from a text, indeed questions whether an author even succeeds in expressing what he intends, I prefer to use an approach similar in spirit to the subject at hand. Hölderlin was clearly convinced that, as a mode of discourse, poetry is able to speak more vitally, more concisely, than other forms of expression. Hölderlin did not question the meaning of the text so much as he worked to establish the meaning of the text as an activity that has occupied man since the dawn of speech. *Text* is a term that can be used ironically, or cynically, especially if one is inclined to overlook the challenge of meaning given by a text; in this sense, since no perfect interpretation or reading is possible, one decides instead to dispense with reading. Proving the ambiguity of a text becomes a challenge, a satisfying pursuit that places the author and critic on an equal footing and, of course, has the effect of absolving the critic of any responsibility concerning the issue of meaning. When the question of meaning is nullified, neutralized, ironicized, the most basic question of study is also blunted, namely: what do I learn here?

This *Hölderlin* is a practicum in reading, just as the poet was a practitioner of his art. What is at issue is the general and specific effect of Hölderlin's poems, that is, how they "work" on us, as indicated in the German verb *wirken.* Some of my colleagues will marvel at my audacity in writing in this spirit on Hölderlin's poetry; they might prefer no reading to any reading that attempts, actually and as lucidly as possible, to establish a meaningful reading. If Hölderlin's poetry, rife as it is with gods and demigods, were not made for mortal consumption, the detractors of meaning would be profoundly right, and the rest of us would desist. But Hölderlin's poetry, gods, demigods, and all, *is* properly suited for our reading and edification. Hölderlin's concerns for poetry were so basic, in the best sense of the word, that it would be cynical to deny access to his poems through interpretation. Those who are still in awe of language, who fear it, suspect it, berate it—but ultimately use it to their hearts' content—should read no further here. For Hölderlin language is as authentic as being, and being is not some trendy notion that could ever become passé.

A Heideggerian approach, I said—but with more than a grain of salt. It is not by accident that a good deal of Nietzsche appears in this study. Since Hölderlin, Nietzsche, and Heidegger together represent some of our best efforts at defining being, it is proper to view their contributions as a continuum. But no one should infer that I am striking a great comparison here; Nietzsche was as different from Hölderlin as Heidegger was different from Nietzsche. And just as Nietzsche turned away from Hölderlin, misunderstanding him as a failed man, a weakling, so, too, Heidegger has read much into Nietzsche that is not there. Let us agree at the outset that each of these great thinkers had his own agenda. When they speak with authority on the issues held in common, we generally benefit.

As the problem of fragmentation described by Schiller, and Hölderlin, only continues to grow, and modern observers learn that "classical" issues are indeed living issues, Hölderlin is more relevant today than he was in 1800. As he himself observed long ago, there are too many sanctimonious poets who call upon "gods" and "nature" whenever they need a good effect. And what of today? For us nature is something of a quantity that we desire, not very strongly, to preserve and protect from the encroachment of industrial pollution and developers. Nature is the green power, it is what reigned on this planet before we took over. And whatever nature is, we seem to be saying to ourselves, it is surely an entity foreign to us. Often it is downright hostile, manifesting storms, floods, and earthquakes, and we reflect on how little has been done to control nature. Perhaps *control* is the key word here. Nature is something we control; it cannot possibly have a hand in controlling us. What emerges with great clarity in Hölderlin's poetry is the extent to which mankind is natural, and the manner in which man is what he is. These concerns may strike some as trivial, while some might argue that they are not the proper challenge of poetry. For the others Hölderlin has something timely to say.

PART ONE

The Work of the Poet

1

The Poet's Role in Joining

Geselligkeit and Coexistence

Variations of the noun *Geselligkeit* occur frequently in Hölderlin's poetry; *gesellig* means sociable or gregarious, but these terms must be supplemented. Perhaps the best English equivalent is conviviality but tending toward the etymology in Latin *vivere*. In "The Oak Trees" (*Die Eichbäume*) the poet explains his attraction for the tall, sovereign standing oaks by first implying that man has to live with nature according to limitations. The poet approaches the oaks from the gardens, "there nature lives patiently and domesticated, / Caring and cared for, together with busy man."[1] These early lines of the poem express Hölderlin's understanding of the necessity involved in man's relation to nature, for nature, which is capable of caring for man, is also cared for by man. The oaks, however, enjoy a different existence: "A world is each of you, like the stars in the sky / You live, each one a god, together in free covenant."[2] The oaks, which elect to stand together, are nonetheless sovereign, having no ties to man; man relies on them for nothing, and they are beyond man both in the deepness of their roots, which grip the earth as man cannot, and in the tallness of their crowns, which penetrate space. The question of sovereignty could well have been on Hölderlin's mind as a result of his relationship to Schiller and his growing discomfort with his reliance on Schiller's support.[3]

At this point in his writing, around 1796, Hölderlin was troubled by the restrictions imposed on him by society, so that *Geselligkeit* does not appear without ambivalence. The concluding lines of the poem are conditional sentences:

> If only I could bear the servitude, no more would I envy
> This wood, and gladly cling to the joining life.

25

> If only my heart, guided by love, did not bind me
> To joining life, how gladly I would live among you![4]

The social aspect of life (*das gesellige Leben*) is not what we understand today as "the social life." In the first sense, it is life that the poet modifies with the term *sociable,* so that for Hölderlin it is in the nature of life to require social contact through joining. Servitude is but one part of that life, and the poet tolerates it for reasons of the heart.[5] The preference that he implies is not for *Geselligkeit* but for the superior existence of the oaks, which stand together yet "in free covenant." This early poem already reveals Hölderlin's basic understanding of the necessity of suffering; he may approach the oaks in order to gaze at them in longing, but he must remain among men, bound for better or for worse to the life that requires company.

Empedocles (fifth century B.C.) became the central figure of Hölderlin's thought during the final years of the 1790s, and the intriguing life of this philosopher provided Hölderlin with the substance for three drafts of a tragedy. Empedocles must have fascinated Hölderlin both as a thinker and a practicing wiseman or philosopher. The four root elements—earth, water, air, and fire—exist in various chance combinations and are motivated by two forces, love and strife. Love exerts a binding and joining force, while strife causes a layering or separation. Hölderlin was primarily interested in the tragic potential of Empedocles, who was a mystic, physician, and active political leader. According to one myth, Empedocles was forced to leave his homeland and committed suicide by hurling himself into Etna.[6]

Hölderlin's great admiration for Empedocles is best seen in the fragmentary drama that bears his name, but the poem "Empedocles" illustrates again the sacrifice that the poet makes for his fellow man. Empedocles, unlike the poet, would not be restricted; his craving for life compelled him into the depths of Etna. The poet honors in Empedocles what he himself craves but is unable to enact, namely a complete union with the earth, symbolizing an act of liberation from servitude that Hölderlin praises as divine:

> Yet holy are you to me, like the earth's power,
>   Which took you away, bold murdered one!
>   And I would follow you, the hero, into the deep
>   If love did not hold me.[7]

Love emerges here as the more powerful impulse, though Hölderlin honors in his hero the insatiable lust for life. There is a fulfillment to be experienced within the framework of coexistence or company, and love is the catalyst. The poem "The People's Approval" (*Menschenbeifall*) begins: "Is not my heart holy, full of more beautiful life, / Since I love?"[8] The poet attributes to his ability to love the power to comprehend the divine in life, while earlier, before love, the people gave their approval to proud, wordy displays of emptiness. When Hölderlin laments in the second strophe that the people only honor what is of value in the marketplace, he associates this popular approval with servitude. The concluding lines voice the poet's capacity for standing in relation to the divine by virtue of having love: "In the divine believe only they / Who themselves are divine."[9] The theme of servitude as one aspect of coexistence is thus juxtaposed with the divine and the beautiful life; man as poet has a responsibility to his fellow man, let us say, the poet is there to ensure that man does not fall into complete servitude. In his necessary relation to others, however, it is only through love that the poet has anything worthy to say concerning the higher life.[10]

The ambivalence toward coexistence seems to lessen in Hölderlin over the years. "Evening Phantasy" (*Abendphantasie*) still bears traces of the restlessness caused by the poet's vocation, but the poem concludes with a peaceful resignation. The necessity for living among others in a meaningful way, devoted to a task that serves the communal spirit by virtue of self-realization as part of the community, is seen clearly in "My Property" (*Mein Eigentum*), where the poet begins to explore what is his by first describing the abundance of an autumn day. The early strophes return to the theme of nature caring for man and man caring for nature, but by now the poet has fathomed his vocation gracefully so that the contrast between the people's realm, namely domesticated nature, and the divine life is not jagged. Instead, Hölderlin praises the man who sits with his pious wife before the hearth: "For, like the plant, the mortal's soul will die out / If not rooted in its own ground."[11] But from this peaceful recognition of the limitations that govern between common man and nature, Hölderlin reflects back upon his property, his essence, and confesses that the divine powers still pull him upward, away from the earth, where man must take root: "Too mightily oh! you heavenly heights / Pull me upward. . . ." And it is here that the poet names his request of the gods; in order that his soul should not long beyond life and become a homeless wanderer, he asks that poetry (*Gesang*) serve as his friendly asylum and the garden wherein he may live peacefully, simply (strophes 10–12).[12]

When the poet speaks of his own proper place, and consequently his own property, as *Gesang*, it is with the understanding that his work must be accomplished here, as if within the limitations of a garden. His appeal is to the gods, and, in the final strophe, to the Fates in particular, but instead of longing for a place among them, we find a realization that the work of the poet is cultivating man's place on earth. Kuzniar perceptively observes that the poet cannot claim too much by way of describing the ultimate presence, for language can also have the function of "distancing God, of descrying the limits within which it can sustain itself. The poet desires to remain within the interim because of the dangers of stepping beyond its bounds."[13] Within the interim, poetry makes the place of the divine among men; the poet expresses a desire to walk among the blossoms of his garden, remaining forever young, but also sheltered from "all the waves of powerful time," in order to pursue his vocation.

Up to now the focus on *Geselligkeit* has been directed to that point of ambivalence that marks the boundary between gods and men, because Hölderlin suffered from this separation but grew to understand the suffering as the higher consciousness of the poet. *Shared existence, coexistence,* and *conviviality* are all terms that designate *Geselligkeit,* but Hölderlin found the gods to be helpful in this regard as well. In "The Homeland" (*Die Heimat*) we find the theme of homecoming; the poet again contrasts his experience with those of others, in this case, returning sailors who bring home their sea harvest of goods, while he brings home only sorrow of love. The final strophe introduces the element of "divine fire" (wine) as a gift from the gods:

> For they who lend us the divine fire,
> The gods also grant us divine sorrow,
> Therefore let it be. A son of the earth
> I seem; made to love, to suffer.[14]

The gift of wine so celebrated by Hölderlin has its divine counterpart in suffering, as love with its emphasis on coexistence has its counterpart in isolation. "The Poet's Vocation" (*Dichterberuf*) begins with a salutation to the god of joy, Bacchus, who came from India "with holy / Wine, waking the peoples from sleep."[15] The first, or instrumental, link between gods and men originates among the gods, for they "lend" their divine fire to mortals, thereby awakening them from a sleep in which there is no relation between mortals and gods. In the same poem, as Hölderlin goes on to lament how man's relation to the gods has suffered neglect and how only the poet is empowered to continue the work of Bacchus (Dionysos), the specific point is made that the Father covers us all with divine night. Hölderlin deals with this period of darkness most creatively in "Bread and Wine" (strophe 2); it is the opportunity seized by the poet to look inward and beyond the affairs of the day, that is, it is the threshold to the world of the divine. Returning to "The Poet's Vocation," however, we find a clear statement of coexistence between gods and men on the one hand, and between men on the other, immediately following the poet's allusion to the Father as he who conceals all with divine night:

> Neither is it good to be too wise. He is known
> By gratitude. Yet he does not bear it well alone,
> And gladly a poet will join others, thus
> do they understand how to be helpful.[16]

Heid's unconcealing - light suspended

In joining others the poet participates in the mystery that descends with divine night, specifically, the poet helps by virtue of joining others. Left to their own devices, mortals could have no inkling of the divine event signaled by the advent of concealment, they would still be asleep, as they were before the advent of Dionysos. Given that the poet helps by virtue of joining others, the poet's vocation would be meaningless without communion. A concept such as *l'art pour l'art,* often ascribed to the period of early romanticism, has absolutely no meaning for Hölderlin; the poet intervenes in the lives of men to share his experience of the divine, to make out of darkness and concealment a teleological suspension of light, insofar as light can only be blinding if it exists without meaning, without gods.

The analysis of *Geselligkeit* in several poems has led us to the poet's vocation, just as Hölderlin's calling crystallized in him with the years. When Hölderlin speaks of the suffering caused by love, as in the poem, "The Homeland," his personal experience with Diotima is elevated to a universal experience of man, for Hölderlin was not satisfied with a poetry that only delineates the personal or describes a subjective state. This evolving concern in the poet as spokesman for humanity is expressed by M. B. Benn in this realization:

> His [Hölderlin's] deepest concern was for the people as a whole, his religious ideal the free participation of the individual in a festal collective worship. The poetry that was to be the adequate expression of this ideal required a form of greater amplitude and volume than the ode; and with the destruction of his private happiness through the enforced separation from Susette Gontard, with the concentration of all his attention on his public interests, it became Hölderlin's primary concern to develop such a larger and grander poetic form. [17]

The celebrative aspect of poetry requires the poet to serve as the priest of the collective, and this matter will be dealt with in the context of Hölderlin's religiosity. Benn quite skillfully points out the advancing nature of the poet's style, with its increasing emphasis on a form suitable for collective worship. The reader of Hölderlin's poetry would be wrong, however, to attribute this aspiration to the failed relationship with Diotima, insofar as Hölderlin had faced the necessity of the collective's relation to the divine at an early stage in his writing; the coexistence of gods with mortals, as well as any meaningful coexistence among men, requires *Geselligkeit*. We have considered the phenomenon of joining in company from two major perspectives; the poet coexists with the divine by virtue of his vocation, but the poet's vocation requires coexistence with the people in order to continue the awakening set in motion by the gods, who lend mankind the divine fire.

There would be little problem in studying Hölderlin as poet if the joining were only a matter of the poet's love for the divine, for that is a given. Hölderlin as the self-reflective poet begins to instruct us when he addresses the issue of the poet joining with the people. At this point the poet must overcome both his great love for the gods and his ambivalence toward the people, who allow their relation to the divine to fall into neglect.[18] No amount of longing, devotion, or worship for the divine will in itself serve as the poet's vocation. In fact, a preponderance of these factors is what stands in the way of mediating between gods and men; because the poet is overcome by the gap, he is tempted to turn his back on his fellow man. The authenticity of the poet's existence can emerge only in the realm of man as the manifestation of the divine among mortals; enacting the bridge between gods and men becomes much more than a personal triumph, for it is the suspension of the personal in favor of enacting the immortal.

2

Faith

Precondition of Poetry

The underscoring of *Geselligkeit* proceeded in chronological fashion, because it was necessary to follow Hölderlin from the earlier poems into those where the theme began to lose its ambiguity. While it was possible to determine beyond a doubt that *Geselligkeit* is in the nature of poetry, the focus was still too narrow for the purpose of exploring precisely how the poet works in the act of joining, and precisely what are the implications for the communities, gods and mortals, once the joining has been established. The deeper meaning of *Geselligkeit* can now be accessed through the analysis of texts that speak in particular to the work of the poet, and this issue will not always be approached chronologically.

A basic attitude of faith is the prerequisite for poetry, in the sense that the poet must acknowledge the existence of something higher than man. "To the Fates" (*An die Parzen*) is one of Hölderlin's most widely anthologized poems; even the title suggests the necessity of faith, for the poet is addressing the Fates as deities who are capable of governing. In three strophes of four lines each Hölderlin compressed a great deal of his own struggle to deserve the role of poet. He begins by pleading with the Fates for one more summer and one more autumn in which to perfect his poetry, that he may die fulfilled. The urgency of his plea is underscored in the second strophe, where the poet explains that a soul must receive its divine justice in life, for the afterlife (Orkus) will offer no second opportunity:

> "And yet, if only once the divine,
> The poem so near my heart, succeeds,
> Then welcome, oh silence of the netherworld!"[1]

The conclusion expresses Hölderlin's deepest conviction concerning the poet's calling: "Once / I lived like the gods, more is not needed" (ibid.). The linkage that cannot be overlooked here is between the divine nature of poetry and the divine nature of the poet's life if only the Fates permit his poetry to ripen to perfection.

The acknowledgment of a higher power emerges as well in "To the Young Poets" (*An die jungen Dichter*), who are given hope in the opening strophe for a ripening of their art: "Only be pious, as was the Greek!"[2] Hölderlin details this advice in the second and final strophe:

> Love the gods and think kindly of mortals!
> Hate intoxication, like the frost! Neither teach nor describe!
> If the Master should cause you fear,
> Ask great nature for advice.

This may be as specific as Hölderlin gets with regard to the role of the poet, and one sees that, more than anything else, the poet is supposed to rely on piety for his instruction. The gods and nature are the higher power, and it is encumbent upon the poet to resist the temptations of intoxication, didacticism, and description. It can safely be assumed that these three elements were prominent in the poetry of Hölderlin's day and continue to seduce poets today. In fact, Hölderlin again laid the stress on piety as the precondition of poetry in "The Sanctimonious Poets" (*Die scheinheiligen Dichter*).

The poets who merely make a show of sanctity are the ones who pay lip service to ancient Greece because it is fashionable. Hölderlin addresses them as "cold hypocrites."[3] The emotional importance of this is seen in the concluding strophe, with its almost resentful tone; the gods should take comfort, their names still grace the poems of the hypocrites, even if the substance is gone, and these poets are always capable of calling on "mother nature" when they need a grand expression. It should be noted that in Hölderlin's day both classicists and romanticists frequently called upon the gods and nature, without necessarily invoking anything but their names; what Hölderlin had to contend with, then, was a readership or a public made callous to precisely those higher powers, which in his case meant invoking not a name, but an act of the divine. One of the most brilliant theorists of early romanticism, Friedrich Schlegel, espoused a view of romantic irony that gained the sympathy of many; in describing romantic poetry as a "progressive, universal" poetry, he stated that "it alone is infinite, as it alone is free and recognizes as its first law that the will (*Willkür*) of the poet shall tolerate no law above itself."[4] Such a view of the poet as the world-positing subject was anathema to Hölderlin, who on this score was not in step with his time.

The devotion of the poet which emerged so strongly in Hölderlin that it alienated him from his peers nonetheless gained him a faithful admirer, the Princess Augusta of Homburg, to whom he addressed a poem on the occasion of her birthday in 1799. The poem must not be viewed as merely an occasional piece, as praise sung for an aristocrat, which after all was common enough. Instead, Hölderlin dared to speak to Augusta as one believer in poetry to another. The personal relationship of the poet to the individual is heightened in characteristic Hölderlinian fashion when the poet associates his praise for Augusta with the act of praising as such:

> Yet my song is glorified in your name; your day
> Augusta! I have the right to observe; it is my calling
> To praise what is higher, therefore did
> the god give me speech and a heart with thanks.[5]

Hölderlin insisted on the divinity of poetry because his faith could not allow that poetry is a closed, singularly mortal act. If the domain of the poet were only society, then the poet would be justified as instructor; if the realm of poetry were strictly imagination, then intoxication would serve. Similarly, if the essence of poetry resided in phenomena, description would be as valuable to man as anything else. The precondition for poetry is the receptive, pious soul, which is given speech and inspiration in the tenuous, ever-threatened relation between men and their gods. The gratitude, which Hölderlin never tires of mentioning in the same breath with praising the higher power, is in one sense humility, but of a rare sort, since only the poet knows such gratitude. Thus it is within the spirit of humility that the poet is given a language of praise, though it will become clear in this exploration of Hölderlin's religiosity that categories such as faith and humility do not operate in all cases as the categories of a Christian value system.

3

The Awakening as the Presence of the Divine

As seen in "The Poet's Vocation," a kinship exists between Bacchus-Dionysos and the poet; the god brought with him from India the secret of wine making, and Hölderlin was in accord with the poets of ancient Greece that the unlocking of nature's treasure through wine making was a gift from the gods. Bacchus's advent is described as a triumph, in his approach he is "all-conquering," bringing holy wine with which to awaken the peoples from sleep.[1] That was long ago, as Hölderlin indicates in the second strophe, directing the rest of his words to the poet of his time: "And you, the angel of day! Awaken them not, / Who yet sleep?" During the time when mythology still prevailed as the worldview, and Bacchus-Dionysos served as the deity linking mortals to their gods,[2] the gift of wine was understood as a link to the gods; it was not taken for granted, but with gratitude.[3] The problem arises with the lapse into which man's ties to his gods has fallen; the poet must now fulfill a role that is beset with obstacles, for the sleep (ignorance, neglect) of humanity is deep.

We recall how Hölderlin explained that the Father conceals all with divine night, "so that we may endure."[4] Guided only by reason, man threatens to become "too wise," that is, sanctimonious, alienated from his instincts, his needs, and his ancestry. The divine night is beneficent, it has a teleology, namely to rescue man from his blindness, in spite of "the light" of reason, and enable him to summon the relation with his gods. It is here that "Bread and Wine" must again be cited.

Bearing in mind that "Bread and Wine" is one of Hölderlin's most formidable works, this nine-strophe elegy of 160 lines will not be given a "total interpretation" in order to keep in focus the element of awakening that is germane to the work of the poet. In the first strophe the poet sets a mood of

34

Geselligkeit toward the falling of night, but already in the second strophe the focus shifts to the individual and to the night, which holds promise as seen in these concluding lines:

> But she [night] must also, in the interval of hesitation,
>> Grant us forgetting and the holy drunkenness,
> So that in twilight something tenable should remain,
>> Grant us the flowing word, slumberless like lovers,
> A chalice more full, and life more daring,
>> Holy remembrance, too, to keep us awake by night.[5]

In the act of forgetting the individual (in this case clearly the poet) is made receptive to "what is tenable," that is, to a dimension of existence that is not transitory like the day and the common affairs of men. The condition is one of holy drunkenness, not mere intoxication, for the personified night fills the poet with its divine liquor, making him capable of pouring forth the word. This sleeplessness by night is the introspection, or superspection of the poet, which makes him more full and grants access to a bolder life, or dimensions of his own life that border on the divine and are not normally accessed. It is therefore that Hölderlin speaks of the poet receiving "holy remembrance" as well, for, in the communion with our ancestry both mortal and divine, the poet remains "awake," receptive, while surrounded by the mystery that is night.

"Bread and Wine" searches in the past, the present, and the future for a point of entry to the world lost to mankind when we allowed the music (*Gesang*) of poetry to die out. Strophes 3 through 6 detail the manner in which the gods first approached us, how we initially embraced them, how the interval, the gap, descended. Much rests on the shoulders of the poet, for, it must be recalled, the gods and even nature have become fashionable slogans. Strophe 7 begins: "But friend! we arrive too late. The gods live, yes, / But over our heads beyond in another world."[6] Hölderlin is not fatalistic; the gods continue, but it is man who refuses to acknowledge the link, to strike the link and celebrate the coexistence. It is a weakness of the times, and the poet is not so naïve as to think he can resurrect a world on his own:

> Meanwhile it seems to me
> better to sleep, than to thus be without companions,
> To wait thus and do what, say what meanwhile
> I do not know, and wherefore poets in paltry times?
> But they are, you say, like the wine god's holy priests,
> Who moved from land to land in holy night.[7]

The conclusion of "Bread and Wine" expresses a hope that cannot be over-looked. The torch-bearer, "son of the highest," is coming; Christ's advent is greeted by the wise, by the Titans, even by Cerberus, guardian to the gates of Hades.[8]

It is consistent with Hölderlin's view of mankind's lapse into sleep that the poet should be compared with the priest of Dionysos, and therefore as the bearer of the cup that brims with a higher life. The wine of old possessed virtues that were readily appreciated by man and recognized as the divine fire presented to man by gods who loved company. But even though wine may still possess virtues that encourage *Geselligkeit,* it is as if the poet alone understands the nature of the link, so that it is his enormous responsibility to serve as the one who conjoins gods and men each time the act of awakening is performed to manifest the presence of the gods.[9] In the eighth strophe the poet refers to both bread and wine in a symbolism understood by Christians, but with a dimension that underscores the benefit of conviviality. The earth, which is man's domain, is a gift from the gods, though the poet is charged with keeping this insight alive: "Bread is the fruit of the Earth, yet it is blessed by light, / And from the thundering god comes the joy of wine." The bread and wine serve as reminders to all that the gods were once here, that they will return "in the proper time."[10] The poet's words, his *Gesang* or hymn to the god of wine, fill the interval with meaning and keep hope alive just as they keep mankind awake. Hölderlin warns that this cannot be an idle pursuit undertaken by "the sanctimonious" poets; awakening the people to their gods simultaneously involves the preservation of the gods' existence, for it is inconceivable that the gods would return to a place where there is no feeling for them, no room.[11]

The poet's *Gesang* could be described as the voice that is heard even in the sleep of mankind, or the voice that continues to be heard when one awakens. Ideally, this voice would be the same one across time, so that different poets representing different ages carry the process along with minimal interruption. The implications of *Gesang* for keeping mankind wakeful are indicated by Eric Santner: "history is nothing other than the story of the union, alienation, and imminent reunion of gods and mortals. The end of this story is the end of history, the end of man as a historical being. The poet's task is to awaken mankind to the workings of this narrative."[12] The "workings" of the narrative I take to mean the constant, creative instruction of man concerning his kinship with nature and other men. This manner of instruction, carried out with the assistance of the gods through Dionysos as intermediary, depends largely on mortals because we exercise volition, we are the emotive beings whose essence can only be apprehended as long as we remain awake.

4

The Gods Are Received

The Poet-Mediator in Revelation

In "The Homeland" Hölderlin expressed some of his ambivalence toward *Geselligkeit,* for, unlike the returning seafarers, he had only a harvest of love's sorrows to show for his travels. Travel and return are favorite Hölderlinian themes; the poet does not fathom the importance of coexistence on its manifold levels without first venturing into the world, for the experience of life beyond the collective nourishes his love for his people and instructs him in the ways of the divine. This is seen in "Homecoming" (*Heimkunft*), a poem dedicated to "relatives," a poem that is brimming with love for the poet's homeland. Viewed after a separation in which the poet has communed with his god, the homeland assumes the significance of invigorated life: "Angel of the house, come! into all the veins of life, / Delighting all at once, let the Heavenly be imparted!"[1] The joy of a reunion with loved ones is an act of consecration, but the poet does not easily, glibly, pronounce the blessing for the festive meal, nor easily express the moment's gratitude. Nonetheless, the poet must prepare to receive the gods when the occasion warrants, as indicated in these concluding lines:

> Often we must be silent; holy names are lacking,
> >   Hearts beat and yet speech remains behind?
> But the music of strings gives each hour its sound,
> >   And perhaps delights the heavenly ones, who approach.
> This prepare, and so the worry too is nearly
> >   put to rest, which came among the joyousness.
> Cares like these, gladly or not, a singer
> >   Must bear in his soul, and often, but not the others.[2]

The preparing that Hölderlin advises is in order to receive the approaching gods, for the homecoming is an occasion that merits their presence. But the poet knows better than any other what the limits of words are, so that he appeals for music to set the appropriate tone for the hour, to welcome the approaching ones. One needn't read *string music* and *singer* literally here, for they are the symbols of the poet's devices. What emerges toward the conclusion of "Homecoming. To the Relatives" is that the poet must make preparations for receiving the gods, as only he knows which occasions will attract them, and by which means they will be welcomed. The specific care of the poet, his concern, is intrinsic to his vocation: setting the tone for the arrival of the heavenly ones, revealing the innermost nature of the homeland, site of coexistence.

Hölderlin expended great poetic energy on the theme of how men receive the gods. In "Bread and Wine" (strophe 5) we read:

> Unperceived they come at first, striving toward them
>   are the children, too brightly comes, too blinding the joy,
> And man shies away from them, a demigod could scarcely know
>   To name them, who approach him with their gifts.[3]

Here Hölderlin drew a transition to strophe 6, wherein mankind, now cognizant of his gods and intent on providing worship, built cities and temples in their names—but the days of ancient Greece are gone, the praising, the naming have fallen into neglect, the gods themselves have retreated. In an earlier analysis of the poem, I indicated that only the poet can animate the gap, only he can reawaken mankind to the revelation of his gods, availing himself of the living symbols left behind, the bread and the wine.

Hölderlin suggested in the last two lines of "Homeland" that the poet's vocation is not always borne without difficulty. Preparing for the reception of the gods requires a vigilance and faith not encountered among the many; otherwise the poet would not speak of "the others." Nowhere does the demand upon the poet, indeed, the danger to the poet, emerge more clearly than in "As on a Holiday," (*Wie wenn am Feiertage*), a poem that Hölderlin did not finish, but which is substantial enough to consider in its seventy-four lines. The poet chose his title well, for the holiday, or "holy-day," that is described is but another day, at sunrise, as powerful nature "begotten out of holy chaos" displays its renewed vigor.[4] The sunrise ignites a fire in the poet's soul: "And what happened before, yet was hardly felt, / Only now is revealed." The poet refers to the work of the farmers in their fields, who are now understood to have been the disguised powers of the gods.

We recognize here the theme of nature caring for man and man caring for nature in a fruitful trust, which symbolizes the intervention of the divine through nature. Hölderlin specifies the nature of the gods' powers in strophes 5 and 6:

> The communal spirit's thoughts they are,
> Silently ending in the poet's soul,
>
> So that suddenly struck, known long ages
> To the infinite, shaken by recollection
> The soul gives forth its song, kindled by the
> Holy ray, a fruit born of love, work of
> Gods and men, bearing witness to both.[5]

The sunrise is a holy occasion, a holiday, because the trust between gods and men that had been established long ages ago once again comes to life. The "communal spirit" is another expression of *Geselligkeit* that enters the poet, so that his song, a work of gods and men, may come forth. But of particular interest now is the manner in which the poet's soul receives "the fruit born of love," namely, as an act of recollection, as an act of becoming struck by a divine ray. Hölderlin had a precedent in mind that goes back to the Greek mythology, for strophe 6 concludes with a recounting of how Semele, desiring to actually see Zeus, was struck by a ray that caused Dionysos to be spontaneously born of her. Bacchus-Dionysos was Hölderlin's principle demigod, and we have already seen how the poet used Dionysos to bridge the worlds of gods and men, of nature and spirit.

The following strophe of "As on a Holiday" is the final completed one, and here the poet's role as mediator is set forth. After the birth of Dionysos, mortals are free to "drink heavenly fire" without danger. But this transference of the divine element to man is not without its sacrifice, for the poet's work demands a relationship to the gods similar to Semele's. Hölderlin explains to his fellow poets that it is their role to stand bareheaded beneath god's thunderstorms in order to grasp the Father's ray with their own hands. The heavenly gift can then be concealed in song and given over to the people, effecting the union of divine and mortal through the intermediary. Hölderlin cautions, however, the poet must be of pure heart and without blame, as the children, so that the otherwise destructive ray does not harm him. The poet's vigilance, his faith and strength, must be great, or else the approach of the god would be too much for him.

Becoming pure as the child in order to be deserving of the gods is a theme that occurs in "Bread and Wine" as well, where in strophe 5 the gods at first come unperceived, while "striving toward them are the children."[6] The fragments that remain of "Holiday" strongly suggest that Hölderlin was drafting a scenario in which the poet might not be prepared for the gods, resulting in his being cast into darkness as a false priest. The authenticity of the poet's calling is imperative, since the nature of poetry itself requires the poet to become a vessel for the gods. "As on a Holiday" illustrates also that the poet is prepared in his turn through his relation with nature, especially where nature and man unite under the auspices of the communal spirit. In this sense, to observe the sunrise on a land blessed with the fruit of the earth can never be a casual, aesthetic experience—it is not divorcible from the phenomenon of joining that is triggered by the prevailing laws of coexistence. The poet does not choose which moment he will glorify, as though the timing and substance of the moment were entirely of his making; so much we learned in the poet's observation of Princess Augusta's birthday. Instead, the poet waits, keeps a vigil, until his own preparedness for the divine invites the approach of the gods, who in turn convey through him only if the poet is strong and pure enough to act as intermediary.[7]

Erich Heller has remarked on a quality of the late hymns, which I observe also in the earlier poems, where Hölderlin speaks of the poet as receiving and mediating:

> At the high, almost mystical, level on which these poems are conceived, the ordinary ornaments and conceits of poetry, indeed the kind of significance conventionally attaching to language altogether, are transformed into something suggestive less of literature than of religious revelation.[8]

Certainly what is at stake in Hölderlin is poetry concerning the nature of poetry, so that poetic language in the sense commonly understood is not to be expected in all cases. Poetry as an act of joining demands the presence of a total man, endowed with the strength of his ancestry and his faith, and therefore the act intends to reveal dimensions of existence with which we have lost contact. Indeed, translators, scholars, and readers alike will often marvel at the seeming audacity of Hölderlin in writing such lines as are found in strophes 5 and 6 of "As on a Holiday"; the syntax cries out for straightening, concepts appear to flash then collide, and yet, to change one word would be to commit the greatest injustice to poetry. If *revelation* is a word that puts Hölderlin into perspective, then let it be so.

Of course, even at its "high, almost mystical level," Hölderlin's poetry does not alienate, for alienation is precisely what the poet's joining disallows. What might bewilder some is the intensity of Hölderlin's faith, that precondition of poetry, which was a motivating force; the poet works in the gap, or he does not work at all. Heller expresses the dilemma: "[Hölderlin's] realization of what the gods have meant in human experience is inseparable from the agony of his deprivation. . . . In numerous symbolic variations this is Hölderlin's dominant theme: how the divine mystery may be known in reality."[9] What the gods "meant" is a revealing usage in and of itself, for it establishes the interval between modern scholarship and Hölderlin, while he was attempting to fill the interval, animate it, as it exists between modern man and the ancients. But Heller is correct, Hölderlin suffered as a poet in paltry times, because poetry, even on the high seat of classicism/romanticism, was threatening to become an "art."

Hölderlin attributed values to the poet and his work that he felt had existed among the poets of antiquity, when it was more rewarding to be a poet because one spoke with the authority and the blessings of the gods for a community. The intensity of the poet's vocation, with its constant vigilance, openness, preparedness, is witnessed in the poet's words. Hölderlin may have been pursuing a reenaction of poetry, and there is no doubt that he was doing pioneer work in the area of poetics; what his ancient predecessors accomplished within the guiding framework of the mythology, Hölderlin strived to accomplish in a setting where even the idea of God had grown lame, and the best poets knew nothing better than to hone their art according to "rules" supposedly borrowed from antiquity. The danger inherent in receiving the gods, in serving as the mediator-conductor of a powerful blast, *is revealed* in the poetry and in the fate of the poet.

5

The Poet's Vigil

Preserving the Memory of the Gods

"**V**oice of the People" (*Stimme des Volkes*) is an ode detailing the relationship between peoples and the gods. The poet begins by explaining that in his youth, he perceived of the people as the voice of god, and still believes this way, for he has learned that what the poet loves does not always do his bidding. This understanding is explored through the juxtaposition of natural situations with mortal affairs; the poet loves the rivers that plunge heedlessly to the sea, obeying a higher command than any the poet might give. The gods ordain all events, and just as the rivers plunge to their demise, just as the eagle will force its young from the nest when it is time, so, too, the long-standing affairs of men are ordained at some time to end.

Hölderlin uses the example of the ancient city of Xanthus to document an event that demonstrates the unswerving demands of the gods and how pious mortals fulfill these demands even if it means their own destruction. Instead of accepting Brutus's offer of assistance as their besieged city began to burn, the Lycians hurled the messengers from the walls. As the fire grew wilder within the city, the Lycians rejoiced at their grim fate and began to annihilate one another. At this point Hölderlin writes: "It is not advisable to spite heroes,"[1] meaning that Brutus's offer of assistance to the people whom he had besieged was construed, heroically, as an insult. But there is more to tell with regard to this horrible event; the self-annihilation was "long since prepared," inasmuch as the Lycians had set fire to their own city four centuries earlier in a war with the Persians, when it became necessary to evacuate the city. At that time also the entire city, with houses and temples, went up as if in sacrifice to "holy Aether."

Hölderlin was concerned less with the spectacle than with the enormity of the loss, but what was preserved in each case was the spirit of the people, which had heeded the voice of the gods. The Lycians had heard of their ancestors' sacrifice:

> So the children had heard it, and surely
> The sagas are good, for they are a memory
> To the Highest, and yet there must also be
> One to interpret the holy sagas.[2]

The saga itself is a meaningful act of communication, passing along information from one generation to the next, so that deeds testifying to the will of the gods are not forgotten.[3] The saga is referred to as a "memory to the Highest" (*ein Gedächtniß Dem Höchsten*), not merely as a "reminder of the gods." Hölderlin chose his words to reflect memory, which is the mortal element, but memory tied to the Highest; this can also be read as the memory (recollective faculty) of the gods themselves. By recounting (*Sagen*) great events, mankind serves as the chronicler, or memory, of the gods.

The poet, in his function as preserver of the tales once again enters at the interval between gods and men, because what remains as the memory is holy, and the divine must be interpreted, or mediated, to the people. Hence the poet's insistence that there must be one to interpret the holy tales. "Interpret" (*auslegen*) here involves all the mediating aspects of poetry, which include receiving, preparing for, inviting the gods, and finally serving as the medium through which the gods speak. In interpreting the sagas or legends of a people, the poet rescues them from mere history; he provides a perspective that gives meaning to the actions of the community. Without this element of preservation, however, the events of the past would not serve a generation in the present, which is to say, the preservation enables the coexistence of mortals and gods in the most basic sense.

The hymn "Patmos" cannot be studied in the present context at any length, but the role of the poet in preserving the mysteries is clearly in evidence. The opening lines are a thesis: "Near is / And difficult to grasp, the god."[4] On the surface this hymn is Christian, for it was dedicated to the Landgrave of Homburg, a religious man, but Hölderlin even here mingled pagan and Christian as in "Bread and Wine." The island Patmos was selected as the title, according to Christopher Middleton, because it was there that "St. John the Divine is said to have written his Book of Revelations."[5] The special significance of John as a seer is central to the poem and alludes to the thesis above, and, of the hymn woven around Patmos, Middleton wrote:

> H. shared the common belief that this John was identical with the apostle John. By an act of astonishing creative audacity, the poem is made to travel in space and time to that region, and on to the Holy Land during the period of Christ's death and transfiguration, thence to the descent of the spirit at

Pentecost. Eventually it returns to the present and future of German spirituality and German song.[6]

I am interested in the conclusion of "Patmos" as the return to the present, which has the most to say with regard to keeping the vigil and preserving a dialogue with the gods.

After the departure of Christ, those who remained behind to give us the Scriptures were "heroes, his sons," engaged in a great, unceasing contest to keep alive his memory.[7] Though the presence of Christ can be seen in all the events of the world since, Hölderlin begins his final strophe with a suggestion of the thesis: "Too long, already too long / The honor of the Heavenly is invisible." But Hölderlin is not appealing for another divine manifestation in the person of Christ; he discussed the reasons why the gods remain "beyond" in "Bread and Wine." Instead, he again voices the concern, which is the poet's imperative, namely, to animate the interval with music (poetry) in order to keep open a place for the gods when they return, as they do periodically, as suggested in the observation of holidays, or to preserve their coexistence with man even though after Christ they are not "visible."

> but the Father loves most,
> Who reigns over all,
> That the solid letter be cared for,
> And the existing well interpreted.
> Thus is the goal of German song.[8]

Caring for the "solid letter" (*der veste Buchstab*) means ensuring that the spirit of the letter, or the spirit of the word remains, and this must be supplemented by good interpretation.[9] "Patmos" belongs among the hymns or "Songs of the Fatherland" (*Väterländische Gesänge*), which is to say that in serving as the poet of Hölderlin's expectations, one does not write poetry for himself or in behalf of some subject of his own choosing. The hymn that praises the gods is, in the highest sense, the hymn of the fatherland, for the poet is the spokesman-priest of his community. *Geselligkeit* requires the poet to speak as the mediator between gods and men, but by the same token, it is the communal spirit that serves as the prerequisite for a coexistence of gods and men. Commentators have remarked on Hölderlin's patriotism and his sense of social responsibility in this context, and these, too, are in evidence. However, when viewed within the context of the poet's special vocation, keeping the vigil and preserving the link are basic acts of faith that give community its meaning.

Ensuring that the spirit of the letter and the vitality of language are preserved has validity far beyond the individual poet's agenda. In the language of contemporary theory, caring for the solid letter means that our relation to the

language

objective world as "that of which we speak," our frame of reference, is not only a fleeting, spoken act, but a translation of the spoken into text. The sagas (*Sagen*) that Hölderlin's poet must preserve were only originally told, and they keep their meaning by virtue of the poet's work in textualizing them. Contemporary debate centers around our ability to extract meaning from texts; there is concern, and, on Derrida's part doubt, that meaning can be coaxed out of a text.[10] Hölderlin seems to have anticipated this concern, as might any scholar who works with ancient texts, and his insistence that the poet should ordain "what endures" ("Remembrance") by preserving and caring for the text, is a statement of faith in the poet's esoteric responsibility.

Hölderlin claimed that the Father loves to see the solid letter being cared for, that what exists must be carefully weighed; at stake here is a historical perspective addressing mankind's foremost activity, namely his use of language. If the language of the ancients is neglected to the point where it becomes incomprehensible or ambiguous, the poets have failed. They have failed not because, in philological terms, ancient texts have become lost, but because the history and prehistory of man is cut adrift from current man. We can of course continue to use, and abuse, language, all the while obscuring the wealth of meaning inherent in speech, but to question the validity of speech as it engages in the activity of determining man's relation to his past, is to undermine his standing in the present. The poets are entrusted with the keeping of text and meaning, so that language does not degenerate into a relative system of random meaning at cross-purposes. There is always the danger in speech that "wrong" or "meaningless" utterances will be made, which is one reason why Hölderlin makes the work of the poet esoteric and why he distances himself from the sanctimonious poets.

Hölderlin struggled to keep alive man's relation to his distant past, to that time when speech was more immediate, less wordy, and gods animated the everyday lives of men. In the process of growing into, of becoming who he is and determining who he will be, man is a partner with language, not a suspicious "user" of it. If language has pitfalls, it is because we put them there, and the simplest way to "prove" that language has pitfalls is to fall into them on purpose. Being and language express man and man's relation to the world; if we want to know ourselves in the world, then language must serve: "A law of fate is this, that each must know all others / That when the silence returns, a language also will be."[11] These lines from "Celebration of Peace" once again underscore the importance of caring for the text; the act of other-knowing takes man out of his monologue and into dialogue, it is a *law of fate*. Other-knowing would be impossible, inconceivable without a language comprehensible to all, such that, even in silence, it works.

The poet serves his community, and the communal spirit we observed in

"As on a Holiday" by recognizing or *recollecting* the presence of the divine, but the meaning of community when shared as it must be between gods and men does not unfold in a vacuum. "Remembrance" (*Andenken*) can be read as a parable on the work of the poet in relation to the community he serves. Hölderlin identifies with the sailors of his poem because they perform heroic acts, make sacrifices that reinforce the strength of community. What begins as a recollection of Hölderlin's days spent in France becomes a study of the communal spirit, for the sailors who venture into dangerous seas, far away from their homes and their loved ones, know better than the others what it means to be separated from the community. We are reminded of the sailors in an earlier poem, "The Homeland," who return with a harvest of goods, while the poet only returns home with a harvest of sorrows. But in "Remembrance" Hölderlin has overcome the isolation of his past, so that he celebrates the sailors and poets as kindred spirits.

News that might be gathered of the world and faraway places is communicated by sailors, who return with "stories," yes, but also with their experience of foreign lands; the sailors are intercultural emissaries. Their unique vocation allows them to share the communal spirit among their relatives at home, but it also forces them to suspend the community in order to live at sea according to the rules of sea travel. Perhaps it would not be too great an injustice to say that for Hölderlin the sailor enjoys a modest demigod status, for he traffics in two worlds. More easily, this could be said of the poet as well.

The medium or element of the sailor is the sea, which of course may symbolize many things. But to Hölderlin the sea is the "source." The fourth strophe of "Remembrance" introduces a rhetorical question:

> But where are the friends? Bellarmin
> With the companion? Many a man
> Shies away from going to the source;
> Wealth namely begins
> In the sea.[12]

The poet finds himself alone, in his reflections, but in his actions he is not alone, for the sailors dare to venture onto the sea. Hölderlin's reasons for naming the sea as the source, and as the place where wealth begins, shed light on the communal spirit. Source of what? we might ask, and what manner of wealth? These questions are answered when the poet describes the activity of the sailors; like painters, they bring together whatever is beautiful of the earth. Moreover, in gathering this beauty together the sailors do not flinch at living in "winged war," that is, they battle the elements, and live in solitude "for years, beneath / The leafless mast," where their nights are not made glad by the holidays of the city (end strophe 4).

The wealth is explained as the harvest of the sailors, the beauty and experience that they gather in order to bring home. If the source still eludes us, then perhaps it is because Hölderlin is not being literal here, nor entirely "literary." The sea makes men fearful, and yet it is the source; the sea imposes a darkness upon man, and yet it is the source. Those mortals who are closest to their gods live in constant danger, so much we have seen in numerous examples from the poet's vocation. The sailors live dangerously, as Nietzsche would say, beyond the safe walls of their cities, and yet they do not shun the city's warmth. The undertaking of the seafarers places them in the vicinity of the gods, the source, and their journey is always an advance beyond community for the sake of the community, as Columbus discovered a new world that expanded the horizons of the old. We must attach great meaning to the fact that sailors live suspended in a hostile environment, or, at any rate, in a place not normally suitable for human habitation. This zone, which Hölderlin designates as "the source," is the well, the unmitigated outpouring of the communal spirit, and we are the fruit as long as we live with the communal spirit at home. It takes courage to approach the source, and, for this reason, the sailor is a special individual. In the same sense, it takes courage and constant vigilance to act as the poet, for, if unprepared for the approach of the gods, the poet will not withstand.

In the final strophe Hölderlin says that the men have now gone to Indians (*zu Indiern*), which is to say they have gone in search of the new world and the fabled passage. The two rivers Hölderlin features are the Dordogne and the Garonne, for they meet and issue into the sea, the starting point, the source. At this point he writes:

> But the sea
> Takes and gives memory,
> And love also fixes the gaze intently,
> What endures, though, the poets ordain.[13]

While at sea, memory of the community is suspended, while memory that goes back further, to the source, is granted. The sea demands a different existence on the part of the seafaring men, but it restores memory of the communal spirit through the sailors, for whom living in the community must be a more precious experience than the land dweller can grasp. Hölderlin has a role for love here, too, insofar as love is the original element of *Geselligkeit* that keeps the poet from wandering beyond his community. The sea is therefore the taking and giving factor, the nurturing element under whose auspices communities arise and flourish, while the poet has the responsibility of ordaining (*stiften*) what endures. The sojourns of man in the territory of the divine come and go, the relation to the gods is costly and complex, but the poet must know how to create a lasting bond, so that, if there is any meaning to permanence, he is the key.

6

The Manifesting of Life

After Nietzsche it becomes meaningful to speak of the philosophy of life, or vitalism, though it can be said that vitalism was a nineteenth-century concept in the broadest possible sense, as I have elsewhere demonstrated in a study of Nietzsche and the poet Walt Whitman.[1] Hölderlin, like Nietzsche, was a student of the ancients, and his encounters with the world of the early Greeks brought him face to face with Dionysos, that symbol of renewed life and resurrection, so that it was impossible for Hölderlin to become a complacent admirer of "dead" culture. The poet in his precarious mediating role is, whether he likes it or not, more alive than others; he must be a strong conduit for the ray of the gods in order to withstand their approach, and he must be strong enough in himself to withstand the isolation demanded of him by his vocation. Hence, in the early poem "Socrates and Alcibiades," we find the poet's sympathy for the philosopher who would not attempt to resist the vitality of great beauty.

In two strophes of four lines each, Hölderlin poses a question and formulates a response, not unlike the three-strophe poems in which he offers the thesis, antithesis, and synthesis. In quotation marks the poet asks why "holy Socrates" offers such praise and favor to this youth; does he know of nothing greater?[2] "'Why does your eye look / Upon him with love, as on gods?'" The implication is that Socrates, famous for his ability to put seeming greatness into perspective, and also famous for his ability to humble his opponents with the dialectic, might be indulging himself in his adoration of the youth. The second strophe dispenses with quotation marks, now Hölderlin will identify with the response:

Who has thought what is deepest, loves what is most alive,
Who has looked into the world understands high youth
And in the end the wise
Will often bow to the beautiful.[3]

Hölderlin draws a parallel between the profundity of thought and the love for what it most alive, for wisdom does not love wisdom but life. In spite of his triumphs in argumentation, Socrates learned to honor that which he himself could not claim, namely beauty, and that which had mastery over him, namely life. We are reminded of Nietzsche's words concerning Socrates' "tragic realization" and how it enabled him, the so-called critic of the poet, to play music in his final days.[4]

The theme is sounded again in "Love" (*Die Liebe*), where this time love is praised as the medium that makes us alive, much as it was praised in "The People's Approval." Hölderlin addresses his readers with a plea; they may disregard their friends, may even, God forgive them, disregard their poets, but they must never turn their backs on lovers: "For say, where else does mortal life dwell, / Now that the servile one, care, rules us all?"[5] In the remaining strophes Hölderlin compares the faith of lovers, their tenacity to life, to the burgeoning spring, which returns inexorably and is blessed by the creative ray, just as it shall be always blessed by the poet's song.

"The Poet's Courage" (*Dichtermuth*) is a strong statement of *amor fati,* an exhortation to embrace life without fear and celebrate existence. The opening line, "Are not all who live related to you?" is the understanding that the poet should take with him everywhere. Ever since poetry (*Gesang*) was conceived, to the delight of men, the poet as singer of the people gladly lingered where many joined together, among those most alive, open and cheerful to everyone.[6] This the poet observes also in his great ancestor, the god of the sun, Apollo, who in spite of his greater stature will also have to face the hour when it is time to depart. What matters, therefore, is the consummation of life, a theme in "To the Fates," and, with this fullest experience of life, the celebration of a beautiful death without remorse.

The manifesting of life cannot occur if mortals strive beyond the limits of their mortality; this lesson Hölderlin imparts in one of his greatest hymns, "The Rhine." Hölderlin uses the example of Europe's important waterway to bring home the point that even this mighty river, born in the mountains of Switzerland and impatient to define its own track, ends up by flowing through Germany and creating a fertile valley where communities flourish. The Rhine is personified as a father of loving children in the cities whom he nourishes.[7] The river does not forget its origins, however, nor the longing of its youth. As things are in nature, so should they be among men, and men who "despise the paths of mortals" are merely audacious.

This theme Hölderlin details in the following strophe by describing how the gods have enough with their immortality but still require one thing more, namely, the experience of human life through heroes and other mortals.

> For because
> The most blessed themselves have no feeling,
> Another must, if it is permitted to
> Speak thus, sympathetically feel in the name
> Of the gods, him they need.[8]

But Hölderlin warns that this need on the part of the gods must not be misconstrued by mortals as a sharing among equals of divine powers, for, if such becomes the case, destruction will befall man. The mortal's life is here given a higher value than men are ordinarily willing to recognize, insofar as man has what the gods cannot have on their own, but such is the nature of coexistence; it still requires that mortal and immortal remain separated, unless of course the joining is undertaken in the spirit of community for which the poet is primarily responsible. It is one matter to live courageously, as the poet or the seafarer or the hero, but it is quite another matter to disdain what must be when the entire virtue of life depends on celebrating what one is.

"The Rhine" gave us an opportunity to look into the theme of working fruitfully within one's limits as a manifestation of life, for, as long as the mortal honors his gods and does not strive to become like them, the gods will in turn share themselves and impart higher life to men. Hölderlin devoted one of his more compelling odes to this theme but with a variation that introduces two orders of gods. "Nature and Art or Saturn and Jupiter" (*Natur und Kunst oder Saturn und Jupiter*) is addressed to Jupiter (Zeus), son of Saturn, who in the chronology of the gods deposed his own father and cast him down into the abyss. The first strophe speaks of Jupiter's success, his unquestioned authority, but already in the second strophe Hölderlin asserts his presence; the poets (*Sänger*) tell themselves that Jupiter had hurled the holy Father, who was without blame, into the abyss. The poets preserve the sagas and tales of the past, and, in this case, the preservation of the event through poetry has ensured that the injustice committed by Jupiter will not be forgotten.

Saturn's rule is described as "effortless," and the poet calls him greater than Jupiter, even though Saturn never uttered a command, nor was he ever named by a mortal. This contrasts with Jupiter as he is presented in the first strophe. It is at this point that the poet asserts himself more forcefully than is generally the case in Hölderlin's poetry:

> Down with you then! or be not ashamed of gratitude!
> And if you would remain, serve the elder,
> And grant him that he, above all others,
> Gods and men, be named by the poet![9]

Jupiter's rule has to be grounded on a proper relation to his ancestry; he cannot rule by force alone, or by "art." This circumstance the poet brings home by explaining that whatever Jupiter has by way of power originates in Saturn, as his lightning originates from the clouds. The golden age that Hölderlin attributed to Saturn was an age of peace, and from this peace "every power has arisen." The last two strophes should be studied together:

> And only when my heart has felt
> What is alive, and what you shaped grows dim,
> And in its cradle, blissfully,
> Changing time has fallen asleep:

> Then I know you, Kronion! then I hear you,
> The wise master, who, like we, a son
> Of time, gives laws and proclaims
> What holy twilight conceals.

Except for the title, the word *nature* does not occur in the poem, and *art* only appears once, in the first strophe, when Hölderlin describes Jupiter's famous "ruler arts" (*Herrscherkünste*). And yet, the poem's first title is indeed appropriate, and Hölderlin expressed his understanding of nature and art by using Saturn and Jupiter as a paradigm.

The injustice that must be repaired before the poet will acknowledge art, and embrace it, is the thoughtless relegation of nature to the abyss, or, the adoption of artistic standards vis-à-vis living, and the enslavement to time. Hölderlin would only have the conscious, modern man, symbolized through art or the art-ificial, remain aware of his origins and the source of all his energy; the servility Hölderlin so frequently laments in his poetry is present here as well, for Saturn-nature ruled and kept the peace without ever uttering a command, while Jupiter-art is a master of commanding without properly acknowledging his mentor.

Lawrence Ryan provides a cogent analysis of the relation between nature and art as Hölderlin understood it. He perceived of the poet's demand for Jupiter to "come down" as a statement of the poet's higher consciousness, for, though the poet belongs now in the realm of Jupiter, he will not tolerate an unconditional ruler without natural piety. Nor, however, will the poet merely long to return to the golden age of Saturn, since at that time no poet could even name the god—pure nature, unconscious nature is not the answer. Ryan speaks of a dialectic between Jupiter and Saturn, initiated at the poet's behest, which allows Saturn's greatness to emerge through the art of Jupiter, the new ruler.[10]

Hölderlin's concept of nature emerging through art was shared by his contemporaries, most notably Novalis and Schlegel. In his *Dialogue on Poetry* Schlegel argued for a new mythology, but a *reflective* one, created by modern man and therefore synthesizing nature and art.[11] But returning now to "Nature and Art," we find Hölderlin asserting his rights as a poet-mediator. He makes his acknowledgment of art conditional on Jupiter's recognition of his natural ancestry and further explains that he will only know and hear the new god when, in his heart, the poet feels that which is alive. "What is alive" appears to be a vague expectation, but it is not when one considers the poet's role in manifesting life. If the wise Socrates could come to grasp the beauty of what is alive, it is even more important for the poet to do so, since his medium is beauty and his vocation requires him to stand at the threshold of nature and art. The poet cannot be ruled by the affairs of the day, his faith and vigilance conjoin the ancient and the new; his soul is animated by nature, and it is taught to sing by art.[12] Hölderlin provided a perfectly appropriate conclusion, however, in his epigram entitled "To Himself" (ΠΡΟΣ ΕΑΥΤΟΝ): "In life learn art, in the artwork learn life, / If you see the one properly, you see the other also."[13]

7

Politics, Utopia?

The Gods Descend on the Fatherland

W hen we speak of *Geselligkeit* as a precondition of poetry and the
poet's role in preserving ancient lore, in preparing for the approach
of the gods, all this indicates the collective, the community, which Hölderlin
celebrates as the poet-priest who receives the communal spirit. As isolated as
Hölderlin perceived himself to be, in the context of his peers and the "servi-
tude" (*Knechtschaft*) of his times, still he argued more strenuously than most
for the necessity of living together peacefully, in a society animated by the
communal spirit and therefore a society awakened to its gods and nature, both
manifestations of the divine. Hölderlin could not divorce his thoughts and
hopes from the events of the age any more than his peers could; in fact, he
held on to the ideals of the French Revolution long after his peers had given
up, long after the political failure evoked its political resignation. In short,
Hölderlin continued to believe.

A prominent commentator on Hölderlin's work, Pierre Bertaux, points to
the political significance of the poet, even claiming that "Hölderlin's entire
work can be seen as a metaphor of the Revolution and its problematic."[1]
According to Bertaux, Hölderlin embraced the Jacobin trinity of freedom,
equality, and fraternity, and added a fourth dimension, namely the distribution
of goods among the people.[2] Certainly the society desired by Hölderlin was
one different than his own, but a society that has room for its gods and lives
harmoniously with nature is not necessarily the society of a political reorgani-
zation, at least, not in the modern sense of *polis*. Bertaux does well to
highlight the political ramifications of Hölderlin's thought, but, whenever the
political strategy is applied, whether from the left or from the right, Hölderlin
ceases to be Hölderlin and becomes instead a prophet of our century's neu-
roses.

53

One of the first serious commentators on Hölderlin was Wilhelm Dilthey, who also saw the significance of world events to the poet's work. Discussing the degeneration of the Revolution, Dilthey described how personal oppression, social pressure exerted by the nobility, and religious restriction emerged triumphant after the Revolution, so that Hölderlin could not manage any exterior success and had to turn inward in resignation.[3] This turning inward in Hölderlin's case, however, should not be regarded as fleeing from society; had he wished to manifest a presence among his fellow poets, Hölderlin needed only to adopt the advice of Schiller and Goethe and become their clone. Instead, Hölderlin's resignation was a removal to a higher plane, a decision to continue the search for a greater society unhindered by the real resignation that lay about him. In this respect I agree with Bloom's observation concerning Hölderlin's relation to Schiller.[4]

Most of Germany's patriots became vocal after 1806, when Napoleon triumphed at Jena and dissolved the Reich. Kleist, for example, and Fichte were devoted patriots, but their attention turned to Germany during its occupation by French forces, and their patriotism inclined toward ridding German lands of the foreign invader. Hölderlin, on the other hand, had different motivations, and his patriotism emerged relatively early, in the 1790s. This patriotism, moreover, grew organically from his reflections on the meaning of community, not as a reaction to hostile forces in his country. Nationalism and patriotism must be separated in Hölderlin's case, for the latter is ancient and all-encompassing, while nationalism is a modern form.

Richard Sieburth remarks in his book on the irony of Hölderlin's fate during the Third Reich. At this time Hölderlin's "songs of the fatherland," or his late hymns, were construed as prophecy for the fascist regime; "Hölderlin became the literary property of the mystagogues of *Kultur.*"[5] There is always the danger, in politics, of appropriating a thinker for the cause, and German ideologues of the Reich were capable of twisting even Nietzsche, the virulent antinationalist, into a glorious precursor. But having claimed that Hölderlin's patriotism amounts to something greater than nationalism, I must now turn to the poems in which this matter is addressed.

In "The Wanderer" (*Der Wanderer*) Hölderlin describes an imagined journey that has brought him through the burning deserts of Africa and the frigid polar icecaps, inhospitable regions that merely aged him. Upon returning to the Rhine, however, everything changes: "Blessed land! no hill in you grows without the grape vine, / Down into the swelling grass rains the fruit of autumn."[6] The poet goes on in this tone of panegyric for many lines, describing a land of rare plenty and tranquility; the sun of the fatherland warms the path before him, he imbibes its light: "Fire I drink and spirit from your joyous cup, / My aging head you guard from sleepiness." Visible here is the theme of awakening, which the poet detailed in later poems, but it is not surprising to see the invigoration imparted by the sun of the fatherland; symbolically, this expresses the hopes that Hölderlin has not yet articulated. The demands on the poet in relation to his fatherland, and the demands on the fatherland in relation to the gods, only emerge in later years.

"Death for the Fatherland" (*Der Tod fürs Vaterland*) is no less panegyric. In battle the just youths, like magicians, fall upon the enemy, "And their songs of the fatherland / Lame the knees of the honorless."[7] The poet longs for a death in sacrifice to the fatherland, so that he might be saved from a mean, common death. He would join the heroes and poets of old below in the underworld (*zu euch hinunter*), and with them learn of the fatherland's victory from messengers; the pagan element evokes even more strongly the ancient *pulcher est pro patria mori*. The fatherland is again a glorious place, but Hölderlin speaks only his emotions here, there is no reflection on the role of the poet.

That Hölderlin was not always convinced of the merit of his people is perhaps nowhere so evident as in the novel *Hyperion*, where his hero makes these observations as he leaves Greece and arrives among the Germans:

> It is a harsh word but still I say it, because it is the truth: I can think of no people more fragmented than the Germans. Craftsmen you see, but no humans, thinkers, but no humans, priests, but no humans, lords and servants, boys and established people but no humans—is this not like a battlefield, where hands and arms and all limbs lie chaotically in pieces, while the spilled blood of life runs into the sand?[8]

At this time Hölderlin had not yet entered the final period of the *väterländische Gesänge,* though he well conceived of it, for Hyperion goes on to describe the people who fulfill his ideal in words closely resembling the spirit of "Germania":

> O Bellarmin! where a people loves the beautiful, where it honors the genius in its artists, there a common spirit blows like the very air of life. . . . Where such a people lives all people have their homeland, and gladly would the stranger linger.[9]

Hyperion's fate, and "Hyperion's Fate Song," the poem that aptly expresses it, are an earlier stage of Hölderlin's conception of the fatherland, but one that accompanies the poet like a warning. Men may go about their business and even excel, but without the communal spirit there is division, and, though we might have every manner of specialist, the human being is not yet there.

In the evolution of Hölderlin's notion of the fatherland there is an increasingly greater role for the poet. Hölderlin becomes more specific on this score in "Song of the German" (*Gesang des Deutschen*). He opens by addressing the fatherland as the "holy heart of the peoples," patient and misunderstood even though foreigners have derived their best from it.[10] The poet laments in the second strophe that, while others harvest Germany's spirit, they mock her as she, vinelike, trails about aimlessly, without form, on the ground. This metaphor is particularly suggestive in light of the significance of wine to Hölderlin's worldview. What the poet laments is the formlessness of his fatherland, which allows others to plunder thoughts and spirit from it because, lacking identity, it remains mute: "Often I wept angrily, that always you / Deny mutely your own soul" (strophe 3). The poet recognizes the fatherland's potential, however, and, by voicing his criticism, he is in a position to restore voice to his country. This aspect of the poet's vocation becomes clear in lines 25 forward, when he shifts his perspective from the fatherland to the children of Minerva (Athena), and claims that the soul of the Athenians still lives. The poet's criticism of the fatherland is intended to spark life in its soul by presenting the memory of the Greeks, with whom the gods had lived in the past.

The Greeks had been struck by the Father's "terrible ray," and, though no longer alive as mortals, they joined with the ether. Hope remains, according to the poet, because, like the spring, "the genius wanders / From land to land" (strophe 10).[11] The implication is that the genius-spirit will now descend upon Germany, and Hölderlin clings to the hope that Germany's silence is a contemplative one that will yield a joyous work, attesting to itself (strophe 14). Two new dimensions emerge in Hölderlin's conception of the fatherland; its potential can no longer be ignored, and the poet must act to prepare it for the approach of the wandering spirit.

"Stuttgart" is a poem dedicated to the greatest city of Swabia, Hölderlin's home. The poet celebrates the autumn in this setting, as everyone, gods and men, converge on the city. The prevailing symbolism of the poem is Dionysian, and in the first strophe we find wanderers approaching their destination with song, and "the holy staff / Graced richly with grapes and vine and / The pine's shade."[12] The thyrsus and the protective shade of the pine indicate the presence of Dionysos, and Hölderlin states the business for which the guests are arriving in strophe 2; this is not the season for care, nor courtship: "Something else is now at hand, now come and observe autumn's / Ancient rite, still the noble one blossoms with us." On this day the individual will be suspended in favor of the community, for the communal god (*der gemeinsame Gott*) Dionysos places a wreath on each head, "And the individual sense is melted, like pearls, by wine."[13] With the approach of the communal spirit, brotherhood will exist among mortals and between gods and mortals.

In strophe 3 Hölderlin names three Swabian heroes of the past, Barbarossa, Christopher, and Conrad; their land is covered with ivy and "Bacchantic foliage." The pilgrimage is continued in strophe 4, after the poet has named his great ancestors, for the poets, too, are beloved of the gods, though lesser of course in deeds. The wanderers are able to see the city (strophe 5):

> For the city wreathed with holy foliage raises there,
>   The glorified one, glowingly its priestly head.
> Magnificently it stands holding thyrsus and fir tree
>   High into the blissful purple of the clouds.

Hölderlin personifies, or in this case deifies, Stuttgart as Dionysos because he is the demigod who joins gods and men as witnessed in "Bread and Wine." His spirit will reign during the autumn celebration, and Stuttgart is the location favored.

The poet is addressing the "great ones," the cheerful ones "who evermore / Live and rule." Their work and creation is done in "holy night," and that work includes the raising up of an expectant people (*ahnendes Volk*). These gods are referred to at the beginning of the final strophe as "angels of the fatherland." The poet is full of gratitude, but he cautions haste: "But the night comes! let us hurry to observe the autumn feast / Yet today! full is the heart, but life is short." The night that threatens here is the "divine night" of the fifth strophe, that is, the natural element of the gods, but, symbolically, it is also the interval between gods and men, and the poet cannot know how long the night will endure before the gods are once again manifested. As the interval, the night is also that which conceals, and only the poet may interpret what "holy twilight" conceals (see the conclusion of "Nature and Art").[14] "Stuttgart" was dedicated to Siegfried Schmidt, a friend who was also a writer, and to him the poet speaks:

> Excellent ones I bring you and the fire of joy will roar up
>   High, and holier will speak the word more daring.
> Behold! there it is pure! and the god's friendly gifts
>   Which we share, they are only among the loving ones.

The autumn feast, which will take place in the presence of Dionysos, the communal god par excellence, gives the poet more powerful speech and purity of word, but the god's gifts are meant to be shared among the loving ones. For Hölderlin these loving ones united in a spirit of community, prepared to give thanks for the abundance of the autumn, are manifesting life in the present; the site of this holiday event is the fatherland. Hölderlin refers time and time again to the Father in a tone of great reverence, and here "fatherland" becomes enriched by the transcendental dimension: the fatherland is where the father's children join together in praise and celebration.

In "Homecoming," which Hölderlin dedicated "to the relatives," the reader witnesses a celebration for which the poet demonstrated his concern about the proper setting in which to receive the approaching gods. On his journey the poet kept a dialogue with god, "The aethereal one seems inclined to give life,"[15] whose substance the poet sets forth in strophe 3:

> Many things I spoke to him, for whatever poets think
>   Or sing, mostly it concerns the angels and him;
> Many things I bid, for the sake of the fatherland, so that
>   The spirit would not descend suddenly, uninvited;
> Many things for you also, who are troubled in the fatherland.

A hope is expressed here, or, actually, a two-fold hope; the spirit of the Father should descend, but not upon a country unprepared for its arrival. The poet's concern for his countrymen therefore goes beyond the concerns of the country, for if they do not possess the grace that is capable of inviting the spirit, "fatherland" is a meaningless thing. This is a revealing concept in Hölderlin's worldview, and one that deserves exegesis.

The Germany of Hölderlin's thoughts is situated during the reaction to the French Revolution but before occupation by Napoleonic forces (1806–13). Since Germany was by no means a united nation with a national capital, as in France and England, there was much speculation about what kind of country Germany should be, especially with regard to the question: republic or monarchy? Historically speaking, the question was answered for Germany by the repressively conservative Metternich era after the defeat of Napoleon. The question again became imperative during the Revolution of 1848, when it became time for the Germans to put forth their best effort toward defining Germany's future. Proponents of German nationhood divided into roughly two camps; the liberals wanted a republic, and their prevailing theme was "no fatherland without freedom," while the conservatives, too, desired German unity but lent their support to the idea of unity (fatherland) first, let the chips fall where they may. The conservatives won the day, and the ensuing political adjustment, not as restrictive as the Metternich influence, guided Germany's course through the establishment of the Second Reich (1871) and on into World War I.

The above detour into Germany's later history is by no means irrelevant to the question of Hölderlin's "political" stand on the poet's vocation. When he expresses concern for his country to be prepared, to be able to *invite* the spirit into its midst, he reveals himself as a spokesman of freedom first, *then* unity through the fatherland. "Unity" without spirit is totally devoid of meaning, as any manifestation of *Geselligkeit* requires the presence and goodwill of the communal spirit. The poet does not express his concern for his countrymen in the manner adopted by Kleist and Fichte during the occupation, namely, as a call to arms. Since Hölderlin was insane by the time of the occupation, we do not know precisely how he would have reacted, as a patriot.[16] One thing remains clear, however, and that is Hölderlin's more inspired understanding of patriotism, which first requires the poet to be in dialogue with the gods as a preparation for making the fatherland worthy of their visit.

More decisively than in any other poem the theme of the spirit joining with the people is seen in "Germania," which is among the "Songs of the Father-land." Though the poet begins by stating that he cannot call upon the gods of old as they appeared in their own land, still he finds the land about him, Germany, to be tense with expectation and longing.[17] In the second strophe the poet explains that the ancient gods had their time; when they begin to disappear, the priest (poet) is the first to be affected, but then the temple, the symbol, and the rites all follow "To the dark land and none may henceforth shine." What remains, however, and what must be preserved by the poet of this day, is the saga (*Sage*) or legend, for it has the power to touch us, and to inspire us with awe. The individual may then intuit the presence of those who have been: "He feels / The shadows of those, who have been, / The ancients, who visit the earth anew." Here Hölderlin speaks of a divine host of god-men (*Göttermenschen*) who will no longer withdraw their presence, for the time has come.

In strophe three we learn that the land lies prepared for them, while from the Aether "The faithful symbol and sayings of the gods rain / Innumerable from it. . . ." The eagle soars again but more skillfully than in early times, seeking among the lands of Europe for joyous booty for the Father.[18] Hölderlin reveals in the next strophe that the eagle is seeking "The priestess, the most silent daughter of god, / Her, who too gladly remains silent in her deep simplicity." It is at the end of this fourth strophe that Hölderlin names the priestess, Germania, and the poet encloses the rest of the poem in quotation marks as the address of the gods to Germany.

The gift to the chosen one is difficult to bear, but Germania has become strong in order to bear it. What makes her identifiable to the gods is the fulfillment of a promise that the gods left with Germania in the remote past. Hölderlin refers to the promise as "the flower of the mouth," and Germany has come into her own by filling the lands with beautiful speech—that is, in Germany the poet was able to preserve the gods. What remains for Germany now is to speak, to become open and assert her leadership:

> O drink the airs of morning,
> Until you are open,
> And name what lies before your eyes,
> No longer may the unspoken
> Remain a secret.

In the final strophe, ecstatic in its jubilation of the new joining between gods and men, and rich with the promise of a new age, Germany's holidays are cited as the fulfillment, the events that attract the gods; as the priestess who invokes the spirit on these holidays, Germany gives counsel to the surrounding kings and peoples.

In the later poems Hölderlin pieced together those aspects of the poet's vocation that contribute to community, so that instead of blind praise for the fatherland, we find expressions of criticism and exhortations to become ready, deserving of the spirit's arrival. In numerous associations with antiquity, the poet reveals his profound faith in poetry as the operative element to any restoration of great spirituality, indeed, to any restoration of greatness. The work of the poet may indeed have political significance, but it is not a political significance that gave Hölderlin hope for the future of his country, though of course there can be no denying that the Revolution as a momentous historical event within the European community played an active role in clearing away cobwebs attaching to traditional notions of "*patria.*" Hölderlin took this clearing as the timely manifestation of the spirit's presence. It was high time someone in Europe focused attention on the question of what constitutes a people (*Volk*), and the plethora of theoretical writing in Germany unleashed by the philosophies of Kant and Fichte, Schelling, Hegel, Schiller, Goethe, and Hölderlin give ample testimony to the fact that German thinkers in particular were devoting much energy to this question.

We recall that in "Germania," at the point where Germany is being told how and why she was selected as "the priestess of the people," Hölderlin explained that long ago a "sign of friendship" had been left behind, metaphorically designated as the "flower of the mouth" (strophe 5). The speech that blossomed in German lands welled forth and streamed forth into all the regions, making Germany capable of giving counsel to all the people (conclusion of the poem). If we accept this generous speaking as Germany's *expression,* we recognize in Hölderlin the spirit of his age as it is described by Charles Taylor in his introductory remarks to Hegel's significance for modern society; the poet for the first time in modern history became humanity's highest representative during the latter decades of the eighteenth century, and expression was elevated to the pinnacle of human value.[19] Germany had long remained silent, a realization that binds Hölderlin's poetry like a leitmotif, but in "Germania" she has come into her own and will express what is hers. This expression, however, is not in the form of vanity but is a sharing.

One of the conclusions that Hölderlin came to in "Homecoming. To the Relatives" was that the poet, not others, had to bear the specific concerns or cares for preparing a setting that could invite the gods. But "the others" are not proscribed from participation in the event, indeed, without them there is no *Geselligkeit* and therefore no communal spirit. The others must be capable of hearing, according to Heidegger, in order to learn from the homecoming poet what it means to be "at home."[20] Being at home, or being in the homeland, logically amounts to being the homeland, but the homeland or fatherland cannot "be" simply by virtue of having a number of people occupying a certain space on the planet. Once the relatives or relations of the poet establish themselves as truly related to him, in a joining, then, according to Heidegger, "there is homecoming. This homecoming, however, is the future of the historical nature (*Wesens*) of the Germans."[21] Heidegger has every right to link the homecoming with the future of the historical nature of Germany because this is what Hölderlin does in "Germania."

The meaning of *fatherland,* which translators such as Michael Hamburger frequently render moot by using *country* instead, can be approached from a philosophical perspective such as Heidegger's, both because Heidegger devoted his own energy to exploring the concept *polis,* and, quite frankly, because he took such an active interest in Hölderlin's poetry wherever it attempts to define that collective through which man becomes most alive, most receptive to the source (nature, the gods). If we attach a conventional political significance to Hölderlin's "Songs of the Fatherland," in the sense that one plays at politics as usual, the poetry will reflect the values of a nationalistic age and represent little more than "Deutschland über alles." If, on the other hand, we try to address the problem through the nature of *polis,* as the root of *politics,* we need not fall into the trap of equating Hölderlin's fatherland with the "state" and with politics as usual.[22]

Through the example of "Homecoming" Heidegger explored the necessary kinship between the poet and the others, those who must become the relatives through hearing, and concluded that the homecoming is the future of the historical nature of the Germans. Let us recall that the poet, in one of his major functions, serves to reveal what is concealed by "divine twilight." "Homecoming" may also be seen in this context, insofar as the poet must reveal to his countrymen the meaning of their commonality, or what Heidegger aptly calls their historical nature. Hölderlin's poet does not contribute to alienation, then; he asserts himself against it and seeks instead to conjoin. The poet in this conjoining role ensures that individuals do not manifest themselves merely as individuals, or, as Schufreider puts it with regard to unconcealment in Heidegger:

> In converging at the *polis,* those individual ways become something more than they alone could be; no longer, as Heidegger answers Nietzsche's lament, "merely poet," thinker, etc., in so far as such individual work takes on reality in contributing to the institution of a measure of "being" for an historical community.[23]

Hölderlin's poet could never become Nietzsche's "mere fool, mere poet" as seen in the fourth part of *Thus Spoke Zarathustra* as the Magician's Song. This degeneration of the poet to the fool, or liar, can only occur within a society that has abandoned its poets and its gods, within a spiritless society. The poet's work in a major sense and the work of all individuals in a broader sense contribute to historical being according to Heidegger, and this is also true of Hölderlin. But the contribution to historical being, which is the essence or nature of what a people historically are, does not come about in a vacuum—it comes about within the community, as the sum of that collective's activity. Hence, when Hölderlin speaks of the communal spirit, the communal god (Dionysos), mortals and gods coexisting and the poet serving as the mediator-celebrant of this life, it is logical to extend the relationship between poet, listeners, and spirit to the site of all this happening, which is, for Hölderlin, the fatherland.[24]

Fatherland was of course also the term used by Hölderlin in referring to his native Swabia. That province or state within Germany is the fatherland in the same sense that Hesse is fatherland of the Hessians and Bavaria is fatherland of the Bavarians.[25] The prefix *father* when attached to locations like *house* or *city* indicates one's origins; German *Vaterhaus* corresponds to one's paternal house, while *Vaterstadt* corresponds to one's home or native town. It is later on in nineteenth- and especially twentieth-century Germany that *Vaterland* assumes the political, nationalistic dimensions that make Hölderlin's poems superficially suspect.

It is helpful to recall what Hölderlin meant by hymns of the fatherland (*Väterländlische Gesänge*). Germania became "deserving" as the voice of the gods, by virtue of her devotion to the word and her prominent role in sustaining a place for the gods. In a letter of November 1802 Hölderlin described in historical perspective the difference between his poetry and the writings of his contemporaries. Hölderlin and his sympathizers were not concerned with providing commentary on or imitating the contemporary poets; in fact, his lack of success measured in these terms owes to the unique character of his poetry. For the first time since the Greeks, Hölderlin claimed, poetry was beginning once again to be "fatherlandish and natural, truly original."[26] This remark should be considered along with the textual evidence of "Germania" and other hymns. To sing of the fatherland is to sing naturally, originally, with the same spirit of authenticity of expression that moderns have ascribed over the centuries to ancient Greek art.

I submit that what many scholars of Hölderlin's work object to with regard to the poet's emphasis on the fatherland is his insistence that the fatherland should be praised or sung. The poet's activity in praising is a vital dimension of the poet's calling. Praising must be considered along with the *telos* that is implied in Hölderlin's conception of the poet. Nietzsche objected to praising, and, justifiably so, with the result that his writings are clearly understood as both antinationalistic and anti-Christian. In *The Gay Science* he wrote: "Buddha says: 'Do not flatter your benefactor!' One should repeat this saying in a Christian church—immediately it clears the air of everything Christian."[27] If flattering one's benefactor, or singing the praises of God, is instrumental in the faith of Christians, then surely that faith would crumble when the element of praise is removed. In praising the benefactor in a religious, devotional sense, one subjugates oneself by introducing a master who is supposedly worthy of praise. The attributes of the Christian God, such as omniscience and omnipotence, clearly imply that praise is in order.

In Hölderlin's case, on the other hand, the praising or singing of the fatherland is undertaken in a different spirit. The fatherland is not an omnipotent benefactor, not a parent at all, but a collective whose attributes reside in the mortally circumscribed activities of human community. The singing is not done out of blind adoration, but as a process of bringing together otherwise disparate elements in order to know the other, and to know community. Since in Hölderlin the *telos* of the poet's activity is to preserve knowledge and a communal sense of knowing, Nietzsche's sharp criticism of Christian praising, subservient praising, does not apply. What is obvious in Nietzsche's writings is that he does not explore with any vigor the notion of a community that draws on its relation to spirit. For all his talk of *Geist*, Nietzsche disavows the possibility of *Gemeingeist* (communal spirit) because he does not accept the values of community. Both Hölderlin and Nietzsche praise man as the locus of meaning, but Hölderlin attempts to make spirit instrumental in a more concrete sense by contributing to a notion of community that arises in part from the poet's ability to "sing" as an act of determination.

PART TWO

Poetry and Ontology

8

The Dialogue as Access to the World

Through Poetry to Being

Hölderlin shared with his contemporaries an urgent concern for the expression of the spirit of man, as illustrated in the poem "Germania," where the poet argued that Germany had served as the most vigilant caretaker of the word and for that reason was poised to receive again the spirit of community that had reigned among the ancients. Expression was not intended in the 1790s and the earliest years of the nineteenth century to selfishly represent the individual, as "one's" expression at all costs; rather, it was supposed to work as a form of participation, in dialogue, in order to join nature and spirit and encourage the unfolding of both within man. This dialogue concept can be viewed as one of the triumphs of romanticism in pointing out the danger of alienation.

Young Goethe had provided a most expressive hero in his *The Sufferings of Young Werther* (1774), yet that hero expressed only himself and managed to alienate himself from society and nature, culminating in his death by suicide. Werther begins happily enough, to be sure; he is a painter who finds inspiration in nature, and he dwells among the common people with a special preference for children, as they are closer to nature than the city dwellers and adults in general. But as a painter Werther never accomplishes much. His expressions are his letters, now wildly ecstatic and life-affirming when his beloved appears sympathetic, now gloomy and cynical when "society" appears indifferent to him and when his beloved cautions that she cannot requite his love. Werther's tragic circumstance is revealed in proportion to his increasing alienation from nature. When nature finally becomes a mirror of his own chaotic spirit, Werther has nothing left to express. He is a failed artist and a failed human being, having succumbed to the self-sacrifice that unrestrained longing and emotionalism bring about in the Storm and Stress hero. But

Storm and Stress, however expressive that brief period may have been (1770s), is a far cry from the later Goethe and Hölderlin. The poet as mankind's greatest spokesman has responsibilities that defy mere individuality in favor of the universal. The guiding thread of Hölderlin's poetry is not emotionalism but thought and proportion.

Novalis's fragmentary novel *Heinrich von Ofterdingen* (1798–1801), written in a spirit of defiance against Goethe's "classical" *Wilhelm Meister's Apprenticeship* (1795–96), is a theory-laden work demonstrating in its form and content the romantic worldview. Heinrich was born to become a poet, but certain vital experiences must intervene before he can come into his own. Foremost among these is the discovery of his beloved, for this union symbolizes not only the awakening of two slumbering souls but also the union between man and the world soul:

> He saw the world in its great and alternating circumstances lying before him. But it was still mute, and its soul, the dialogue, not yet awakened. Already a poet was approaching, hand in hand with a lovely girl, to unlock the hesitating lips with the sounds of the mother tongue and the touch of a sweet, tender mouth, unfolding the simple accord into infinite melodies.[1]

These lines are reminiscent of the significance of love, and the beloved, to Hölderlin's vocation. To speak of the world's soul as dialogue requires the logical pursuit of the metaphor to the poet, who not only represents language as communication, or language as everyday speech, but language in the highest sense of art, a function of manifesting the spiritual among men and revealing, as Hölderlin wrote in "Nature and Art," what "holy twilight conceals."

Novalis once again established the link between mortal intimacy and dialogue with the world by offering an explanation of the psychology of communication; language itself is a microcosm of symbols and sounds, and man desires to master the world in the same way he desires to master his language and freely express himself in the world. The origin of poetry, therefore, lies in the joy experienced by man when he manifests in the world what lies beyond it; indeed, this ability is "the original drive of existence."[2] It should not surprise anyone that Novalis ascribed such an original, or underlying status to language, for in his view of being, the world at large needed to be "romanticized," that is, revealed in its fascinating multiplicity precisely through the poet's intervention in everyday reality, which is powerless to convey being. Hence, as Novalis stated in one of his many fragments: "Poetry is that which is genuinely, absolutely real."[3]

Novalis's contemporary and collaborator Friedrich Schlegel also had much to say on dialogue, not only as a form of expression requiring *Geselligkeit* but also as the instrument to reveal being, and his views emerge in another milestone work of theoretical romanticism, *Dialogue on Poetry* (1800). It is in this work, closer to Hölderlin in conception because of Schlegel's reliance on ancient Greek culture, that a "new mythology" was called for which would reflect modern man's greater reliance on reason.[4] In Schlegel's view, poetry and philosophy had only become separate disciplines in the modern age, and poetry (*Poesie*) should reunite them. Schlegel's conception of the poet diverges from Hölderlin's insofar as it grants primacy to the will of the poet, so that it will be more useful to return to the dialogue as such in order to pursue its implications for poetry.

Heidegger has written extensively on the language of everyday usage versus the language of poetry.[5] He is in a position to inform us on the nature of poetry as dialogue due to his own philosophical writings in the area and of course his great interest in the poetry of Hölderlin. If language is something that calls or summons into being, it is to be expected that this authentic calling of language cannot occur within the restrictions of everyday superficiality. On this score Heidegger seems to agree with Novalis that the mastery of language is a basic human drive striving toward being. If one searches for the language in which a calling can still be heard, one must turn to poetry; it is here that man is challenged in his "use" of language, effectively brought out of his everydayness into a region where his relation to other beings and the world is made clear.[6] Judging by this paradigm, which appears to follow very closely Hölderlin's perception of poetry, the more "everyday" poetry becomes, the more insurmountable grows the interval between man and his spiritual dimension, or, as Hölderlin puts it, between men and gods. The calling of which Heidegger speaks is a dialogue, for calling must address itself to someone, to something, and is not undertaken without the expectation of a response.

It is often remarked upon among scholars that Hölderlin was for a time the close friend of both Schelling and Hegel, two individuals who distinguished themselves as philosophers. The 1790s were years of theoretical speculation in which novels, essays, drama, and poetry reflected a celebration of writing, but the philosophically oriented Hölderlin demonstrated a preference for poetry as opposed to philosophical writing. In so doing, however, he was not embarking on some aesthetic sidetrack; we have had occasion to observe that the vocation of the poet is indeed down to earth and that Hölderlin's concerns were not primarily for himself but for the community that he hoped to serve. Hölderlin chose poetry as his manner of discourse, his manner of expression, for reasons that had less to do with "choosing" than with fulfilling a vocational promise that was also an existential imperative.

Paul de Man speaks of the relation between true understanding and totality; one may become "lucidly aware" without, of course, ever reaching total understanding as long as the individual represents a form. In this sense, one is reminded of Hölderlin's emphasis on remaining awake, on manifesting life in the everyday while striking a link with the spiritual ancestry, which is capable of culminating the everyday as holiday. De Man continues to speak of poetry: "The fact that poetic language, unlike ordinary language, possesses what we call 'form' indicates that it has reached this point. In interpreting poetic language, and especially in revealing its 'form,' the critic is therefore dealing with a privileged language; a language engaged in its highest intent and tending toward the fullest possible self-understanding."[7] As a poet who voiced his concern for the possibility of poetry in his own age, Hölderlin was also a critic, and, in any case, he was a philosopher. But poetry as it is represented by Hölderlin is, first and foremost, poetry; what seduces the critic to apply additional categories to this poetry is the fact that, when compared to other poets or when regarded historically among the world's poets, Hölderlin has more to say than the critic generally "allows" poetry to say.

Since Hölderlin and his contemporaries viewed poetry as a catalyst for dialogue, questions must be asked concerning the nature of the "other" or "others" who take part in the dialogue. Historically speaking, Hölderlin had more to say concerning the character of the dialogue in relation to being than any other, for while his romantic peers called for a dialogue (new mythology) and attempted to place poetry at the vanguard of a cultural movement synthesizing elements of the past with man's later achievements in the field of rational philosophizing, still very little remains of the romantic paradigm with regard to clarifying being. On one point in particular the romantic contemporaries were weak, namely, in demonstrating the value of the ordinary, or the common, in relation to the romantic sublime. Often for them it was a matter of reforging the ordinary into the extraordinary (Novalis) or climbing beyond the mundane into a stratosphere of pure imagination (Hoffmann's emphasis on *Fantasie*); yet Hölderlin addresses the issue of what it means to be, in relation to others and in relation to the world at large, in terms that accommodate not only the romantically favored artist but all who "toil below." And though Novalis expended much energy in defining the poet's role as the role of the priest, a reader is able to observe a much stronger willingness to serve as the mediator in Hölderlin, as well as a much stronger love for the here and now.[8] *Geselligkeit* is a precondition of poetry, and the poet occupies an often precarious place on the threshold of his everyday world, for this everyday world is precisely the one that must receive the gods, and the poet must ensure that his people are ready. Hölderlin specifically names the dialogue in several of his poems; by analyzing what is meant in each case, we can determine something about the nature of our dialogue partner, the other, and, in so doing, focus also on the dialogue's contribution to being.

Höl-
Relation
what it means
to be
here & now

"The Poet's Vocation" has already been cited in connection with earlier themes associated with the poet's work, and we can return to this centrally important text for clarification of the dialogue concept as well. Hölderlin began the poem with the image of Bacchus, "god of joy," coming from the East to awaken the peoples from sleep with his holy wine; from here the focus is on the poet of our age and on the relative godlessness with which modern man probes into the heavens and assumes to know all through the power of reason. But Hölderlin warns that the Father covers our eyes with holy night *so that* we may endure; the all-important nightfall of "Bread and Wine" is given to us in order that we have opportunity to establish contact with the spiritual ancestry, the greater community, which includes man and gods, spirit and nature. The penultimate strophe of "Vocation" returns to the theme of knowledge for its own sake and the danger of adopting false wisdom in such a way that the poet, with his gratitude for and knowledge of the divine, is the one who keeps the link between man and gods open. This condition is evident where Hölderlin writes that the poet's special gratitude, and his special relation to the divine, is not easily borne *alone,* so that he gladly seeks the company of others who are themselves helped by the poet even while he is helped in the act of turning to them.[9]

If the poet's relation to the gods were strictly a selfish matter, then the term *dialogue* would not be in order, for the individual who enjoys, or imagines he enjoys, a relationship with the gods that is justified in and of itself would still be a total outcast. Hölderlin frequently describes the gods and the primary demigod Dionysos (Bacchus) as joining forces, as beings who do not live for themselves but desire the company of mortals; it is for this reason that the holy fire of wine was given to men by Dionysos, as expressed in "Bread and Wine" and other poems. The poet's gratitude makes him sing; it makes him express nearness to the divine and preserve legends in which man's relation to his gods give testimony to both. Just as the presence of the gods can be overpowering, like a bolt of lightning that only the genuine poet can receive and transmit to his listeners, so, too, the holding-in of the poet's gratitude would be a meaningless act, or an act in defiance of his vocation. Instead, the poet joins with others and is helped to impart his gratitude, so that the joining acts as a natural and desired dissipation of energy from the source to the people. The people are also helped, of course, in this act of joining, for a true dialogue can only be where man is in contact with all his faculties. In "The Poet's Vocation" the dialogue is enacted on four levels of communication; the gods serve as the source, the first instance, and they present man with the holy wine of Bacchus, second instance. The poet of today must serve as the third instance, continuing the work of Bacchus, and, finally, the poet's listeners, the others joined by the poet, complete the circuit.

One of Hölderlin's greatest hymns or *väterländische Gesänge* is without doubt "Celebration of Peace" (*Friedensfeier*), and the poem has inspired more controversy than any other among Hölderlin commentators. The timing of the poem led some to conclude that the occasion was the Treaty of Lunéville (1801), and therefore the guest summoned to the celebration by the poet is Napoleon Bonaparte, while the landscape described is supposed to be Hölderlin's native Swabia, which he hoped would become a separate republic.[10] There are, to be sure, compelling arguments on both sides, but I think the Christian/pagan thematics are characteristically in evidence and, therefore, see in "Celebration of Peace" yet another treatment of a demigod, as in "The Poet's Vocation" and "Bread and Wine." The demigods Dionysos and Christ were of especial importance to Hölderlin's conception of the divine for reasons that I hope have become clear, and the poem at hand offers us ample opportunity to explore the nature of dialogue.

Hölderlin suggests the dialogue very early, in fact before the poem begins, in his unusual preface, which addresses the reader straight on. He pleads here for an understanding of the poem, which might strike some as unconventional because of the language used, and, after claiming he "could not do otherwise," Hölderlin wrote: "On a beautiful day almost any manner of song can be heard, and nature, from which it springs, also takes it back again."[11] The poet seems to be saying that a beautiful day is itself an invitation to song (poetry), since after all we are perceiving not the individual poet but nature speaking through him. This context calls to mind "As on a Holiday," and any day of the world in which the communal spirit is manifested is indeed a holiday. When the poet says he cannot write otherwise, he means it literally, for nature has provided him with the song, just as the poet's gratitude so frequently compels him to praise. Hölderlin has begun the dialogue by prefacing his poem with a hint that sets the mood for the arrival of the honored guest; the readers should not think that the poet is expressing some idiosyncratic preference here, for the "prince of the feast" designated in strophe 2 has already been placed in the highest company of man and nature joining in a dialogue of celebration.

It is in the seventh strophe that Hölderlin explains the logic behind the advent of Christ, who in the previous strophe is described as the son of God who teaches us how to observe holidays. Observing holidays is, as we have learned from other Hölderlin texts (notably "Stuttgart" and "Homecoming"), the act par excellence of communality, in the here and now, while it also preserves a space for the gods. The description of God in strophe 7 requires us to hark back to "Nature and Art, or Saturn and Jupiter," because of these opening lines: "For long ago he became too great to be lord of time, / And far extended his field reached, but when did it exhaust him?"[12] What it means to be lord of time was treated in "Nature and Art" because Saturn was god of the golden age, who ruled without commanding, effortlessly, by virtue of his greatness; Jupiter however, must acknowledge that he is a son of time and thereby honor his father before the poet can acknowledge him and his new rule. The Christian God referred to in "Celebration" has likewise been a factor for so long that he does not rule, or act as "lord of time," meaning his role is not exhausted in the temporal.

But the unique quality of Hölderlin's conception of the divine is that it requires us as much as we require it; the gods of whom the poet speaks can only *feel through man,* as expressed in "The Rhine," and by feeling vicariously in behalf of the gods, all mortals are endowed with an experience of greater vitality. It is therefore characteristic of Hölderlin's conception of the divine that, unlike the traditional, perhaps Christian, view, it is not metaphysical but very much in evidence right here. This centrally important dialogic aspect is seen again in "Celebration":

> But once even a god may choose a workday,
> Like mortals, and share all aspects of fate.
> A law of fate is this, that each must know all others,
> That when the silence returns, a language also will be.[13]

Hölderlin completes the image of the god electing to share in man's fate by describing how the Master, having completed his image, is transfigured by it and steps out of his workshop and into our experience. At issue here is the dialogue that must be if "gods" or "divine" have any living meaning; surely a god, requiring the company and faculties of man, would be remiss if he did not complete himself in order to then step out of his own realm and into ours—could there be "completion" within the closed circuit of the god sitting alone, hidden, inaccessible, enigmatic?

The law of fate demands that everyone will know (*erfahren*) everyone else—which is to say, there can be no separation, all will be in communication. This statement of interconnectedness applies to gods as well as men, and in the silence there will also be a language. A language that governs in the silence may be interpreted symbolically in an "inner language," or perhaps the metalanguage of the romantics, but here Hölderlin means otherwise. In spite of any silence, or in spite of what may not be spoken, the law of fate imposes language, a dialogue of other-knowing. This dialogue of other-knowing is being.

The return of silence, which may be a brief interval or the greater interval that caused Hölderlin to frequently lament the loss of the divine is therefore animated by speech—let us say, in a manner consistent with the fall of night in "Bread and Wine" and the flood of poetry that is released. "That each must know all others" (*Daß alle sich erfahren*) is a strong indication that the poet, though instrumental in bringing forth the dialogue or creating the scene for it, nonetheless does not share a privileged, isolated relation to the gods. If we accept the other-knowing and its attending language as a state of being that embraces all beings, then Hölderlin's dialogic thinking reaches beyond the poet-listener relationship. The language enabled by other-knowing need not be poetry as such, since the condition fostered by other-knowing is not strictly verbal-communicative. Hence, we find so often in Hölderlin that "the others" are quite simple people, not necessarily listeners to the poet but then again, having in common with him a gratitude and spirit of communality that clarifies their being. In this context Hölderlin held the plowman, sailor, merchant, soldier, mother, and all lovers in the most general sense as equal participants in the dialogue that characterizes being.

The reciprocity inherent in the dialogue emerges forcefully in the eighth and ninth strophes of "Celebration." Strophe 8 begins:

> Much from morning on,
> Since we have been a dialogue and hear of one another
> Has man learned; but soon we will be song.[14]

The poet designates morning and thereafter as a beginning of the dialogue, and man has learned, experienced, much (*erfahren*) since then, indicating that being has been clarified during this time. The reciprocity between men and gods occurs during this time through the observance of the feast day, which the poet calls "The token of love, the testimony / That you are still holy to us." The feast day bears special significance as seen in strophe 9; it is

> The all-assembling, where heavenly ones not
> Through miracle, nor unseen in storms are manifest
> Where rather joined hospitably together in song,
> Present in chorus, a holy number
> The blessed ones in every manner
> Are together, and their most beloved also,
> To whom they cling, is not missing; therefore I called you
> To the banquet, which is prepared,
> You, unforgettable one, you, at the evening of time,
> O youth, to the prince of the feast. . .

The feast, which is described as "all-assembling" (*der Allversammelnde*), already features the heavenly beings together in hospitable circumstances, "in every manner," and there is song. Earlier Hölderlin had written that the dialogue that has brought us much since the morning of the world will soon be song, so that from one state of being we will embark upon another. The prince of the feast presents the occasion for gathering, but the poet continues to develop the dialogic aspect by claiming, in the concluding lines of strophe 9, that "our species" (*unser Geschlecht*) will not sleep until all those beings who have been prophesied, all the immortals, reside with us in our house and speak to us about their heaven.[15] In this context gods dwelling or visiting with men, speaking to one another, provide a nontranscendental manifestation of the divine. The fact that Christ is summoned to the prince of the feast or to the guest of honor is especially appropriate, since, as a demigod, he joins the otherwise separated realms in one being. Christ is summoned to the feast at the "evening of time" as a further indication of a new state of being enabled by the reciprocity between gods and men; mankind's being as a dialogue is to become song, introducing an additional dimension that corresponds roughly to the analogy existing between everyday speech and poetry. The evening of time reminds us strongly of the thematics of "Bread and Wine," wherein evening and night open a portal to higher being, but this evening must also be thought in connection with the morning signaling mankind's collective being as dialogue. From morning to evening there is consummation of being, and therefore we can turn to sleep only after having experienced being as both mortal and divine.

We have considered "Remembrance" in a variety of contexts, as one of Hölderlin's near-perfect meditations, and now return to it with a focus on dialogue. Prominently featured are the sailors who return to the source and gather "the beauty of earth," while at home people observe their holidays with music and dance. But before Hölderlin lets his poetic vision wander to the sea, he sketches in three strophes of exquisite lyrical balance the unfolding event of the landscape in France, to which his remembrance has transported him. The movement of the poem is in keeping with the opening line "The north-east wind blows." This wind promises "fiery spirit" and good sailing, and with it Hölderlin's journey into remembrance begins. In a panoramic sweep Hölderlin passes the Garonne, the gardens of Bordeaux, a plunging brook, and a pair of oaks and silver poplars looking on. The event is continued in the second strophe, with a description of the elmwood inclining toward the mill, and a fig tree growing in a yard. He describes how in that place tanned women walk, in March, "when equal is night and day."[16] The otherwise passive scenes are given animation through the use of carefully selected verbs, just as the poet allows nature to express itself in actions in "Half of Life" (*Hälfte des Lebens*).[17] The event of re-presenting himself with a living past is in keeping with the poet's expressed wish in strophe 3; he asks for the fragrant cup "full of dark light" in order to rest. If we take this fragrant cup to be filled with wine, which is dark light because the holy quality of wine equalizes or reconciles day and night, then the poet is on the verge of entering a new phase of remembrance:

It is not good,
To be soulless with thoughts
Only mortal. But good
Is a dialogue and to speak
The heart's opinion, to hear much
Of days of love,
And deeds which happen.

The dialogue idea introduced here posits the existence of something greater than mortal thoughts, which have no soul unless the mortal is joined with the other. The other is suggested in the remaining two strophes, for it is here that Hölderlin asks: "But where are the friends?" The ensuing discussion of the sailors who go to the source is the lyrical device by which the poet reaches the highest level of remembering as an event manifesting being. Viewed in this context, everything in "Remembrance" contributes to the dialogue in an active way, and the process of remembering contributes to that which endures, as indicated in the final line: "What endures, though, the poets ordain." Hölderlin has placed the dialogue at the threshold of the event of going to the sea as to the source of being.

Hölderlin's conception of the dialogue bears certain puzzling features. On the one hand, he seems more sensitive to the necessity for including *everyone* in the dialogue than most poets of his age, while on the other hand, the poet is prominently featured whenever the dialogue occurs as event. It is the poet who summons Christ to the feast in "Celebration," and already this act signals the poet's central importance in preparing a place for the approach of the gods. But the poet is never alone with the gods, and he observes that it is not good to be without soul, concerned only with the mortal. Earlier I suggested that Hölderlin's poet shares a demigod status because of the extent to which he works as a mediator between gods and men, but clearly Hölderlin attached value to gods and demigods only insofar as their operations are conjoined with the everyday chores of being human and contribute to the clarification of being. In order to illuminate the unique contribution Hölderlin makes to the clarification of being through dialogue, I will conclude with an analysis of a central Nietzschean idea concerning being and will allow Hölderlin's treatment to emerge through comparison.

In Nietzsche the overman (*Übermensch*) represents that higher state of being that man will achieve when his spirit catches up with the evolution of his body. In this sense it is easier to understand his emphatic claim that there has never yet been a natural man and that we must work toward this goal; it will require the demythification of nature.[18] Man's being is his own responsibility, an idea that Nietzsche discussed using the analogy of the clay and the potter. The unique thing about man among all beings is that he is his own clay and his own maker; we may create ourselves, or we may leave it up to others to shape and mold us—we remain clay. But man as creator works on himself and moves from creature-creation to creator; culturally speaking, if the obstacles of life are removed and man has nothing to surpass by way of self-creation, then the possibility for man taking control of his own being is threatened.[19] This is where the oppositional nature of Nietzsche's thought enters, for very little can be accomplished within the community, and Nietzsche's "creator" must always find another obstacle to overcome.

The prophet Zarathustra had much to say on being, and in a very inspired way. This is a passage from "On the Blessed Isles":

> Once man said God, when he looked upon distant seas; now
> however I taught you to say: overman.
> God is a conjecture; but I want that your conjecturing
> not reach further than your creative will.
> Could you *create* a god?—Then be silent about all gods!
> But well could you create the overman.[20]

Nietzsche looks at being as unrealized potential, but this potential can only be accessed by man, in an act of self-will, with a primary stress on creation. In Nietzsche creation is the freedom to become greater, stronger, and less dependent, that is, it is the freedom to evolve toward overman.

Under the same heading in *Zarathustra,* the attack against gods is continued with vehemence: what would there be to create if there were gods? Instead, Zarathustra explains that this creative will drives him to seek out the true image of man as if he were a stone mason hewing that image out of a block of stone. The block of rough stone represents man's condition of imprisonment to his ideals, but the creator must master this situation to liberate the image of natural man. After all, mankind was said to have been created in the image of his god, and this attitude of self-deprecation has become so firmly entrenched that any other image of man appears almost inconceivable. This accounts for the vehemence of Nietzsche's campaign against not only Christianity but "gods" in general. If there is greatness in man, according to Nietzsche, it shall be forged in the trial of his own self-overcoming, without any help from beyond and in the face of his uninspired, "rabble" community at home.

Returning now to Hölderlin's notion of being as dialogue, we realize how generous it is, and how nonidealistic it is in spite of' appearances. For Nietzsche could well rage against the ordinary man and his institutions, especially his religious sentiments, as long as only the creator has any chance for authentic being. Being in Nietzsche is a fate that must be earned not through communality but *against* it, and insofar as the communal spirit of man encourages other-knowing and the other is also divine being as a reciprocal relationship between men and gods, Nietzsche had to do away with gods and reciprocity. Only the willing creator emerges from the darkness in Nietzsche, but the overman is also one of those damnable ideals, albeit the ideal of the anti-ideal.

This brings us now face to face with Hölderlin's gods and to the question: are the gods created by man, as illusions, or are they a manifestation of being that cannot be separated from man? Hölderlin had every right to speak of gods as real beings since he does not insist upon the traditional division or duality that makes gods mere ideals. Furthermore, the dialogic nature of being gives each his due and gives credit to everyone as participant in the dialogue, not in some detached world of the beyond but here and now. The "law of fate," which holds that all must know the other, is a necessity of being, not an arbitrary stance in defiance of a particular mode of being. In Hölderlin the gods cannot be the enemy of man because they enable being through the dialogue, and this being brings man into the region of living that is most real, most authentic, and most vital. It is easy enough to understand that Nietzsche attacks the gods because he grew convinced that vital energy was being expended on the preservation of chimera, but his conviction has more to do with his definition of being as *not sufficiently mortal* than with the issue concerning the authenticity of gods and their roles in being. By "not sufficiently mortal," I mean that Nietzsche holds man culpable for casting mortality in a negative light vis-à-vis immortality. Nietzsche's early statements on the "all too humanness" of man become an affirmative stance when he launches his campaign against idealism and romanticism, which act as drains on authentic human endeavors. Hölderlin, too, aspired to an authentic being, but he did not exclude the gods or the common man from his perceptions. It may be that Hölderlin's celebration of life as communal gathering is every bit as illuminating, and far more likely to be achieved, than Nietzsche's Promethean solitude of the creator.

The expression of being through dialogue is a breaking through to the communal spirit, and this event also indicates a willingness, indeed a necessity among men to discover themselves in the company of others and within the bounds of what is. What Hölderlin frequently criticizes, and sometimes laments, is the godlessness, or soullessness of existence, which strips life of its meaning and saps us of spirituality. As a species, we already are more, are greater, than is ordinarily apparent, and the dialogue ensures that we do not nod off to sleep. As opposed to the moral categories by which Nietzsche judges man to be a nonbeing, since *anti-moral* is still tethered to morality in the same way that *anti-ideal* remains tied to idealism, Hölderlin exhibits a patience for what men are and holds man in very high esteem, since his gods must be in the here and now in order for the dialogue to work to man's benefit. And it is here that the fundamental difference between Hölderlin and Nietzsche must be explored; Hölderlin allows for a dimension of being that man does not create, but in which man takes part, while Nietzsche grounds being unconditionally on the mortal, thereby driving a wedge between men instead of accessing being through collectivity. But here we are approaching the border of the analysis of being as dialogue, and the exploration of Hölderlin's conception of the divine lies ahead.

9

Nonmetaphysical Divinity?

Being's Dispensational Aspect

Throughout Hölderlin's poetry one finds references to the divine, to the gods, to God, to heavenly ones, to demigods—it is enough to confuse the most persistent analyst and to call forth such reactions as we found in Nietzsche's *Zarathustra* vis-à-vis gods. And yet, one of the poet's most alluring qualities is his ability to speak originally on the nature of the divine, "original" taken here to mean the basic, the source, with regard to a dimension of being that no study of Hölderlin can afford to treat lightly. Up until now my method has been to take the poet at his word concerning expressions that touch on the divine—that is, significance was attached to that concept primarily within the multiplicity of contexts in which it occurs. This procedure has the advantage of exposing the reader to texts in which the divine is cited, so that a familiarity is already in place now that the particular issue of the divine must be treated.

Within the context of love as it contributes to *Geselligkeit,* "The People's Approval" was discussed because in this poem Hölderlin claimed that his own heart became holy and full of life only since he loved. Though the poet had been "wordier" and less restrained before his love blossomed, he was nonetheless emptier then. The crowd, he lamented, likes what is dished up in the marketplace, while "In the divine believe only they / Who themselves are divine."[1] It would be easy to accept these words at face value, since the poet draws a distinction between one who loves and one who for other reasons might appeal to the crowd. But if we think in terms of the poet's own insistence on a dialogue as the expression of being and follow the dialogic thinking to its inclusion of *mortal, nature,* and *divine,* then it emerges that the concluding lines of the poem say more; those who believe in the divine are themselves divine because they also believe in themselves. Hölderlin is not

80

merely stating his own piety for the record; instead, he is making belief in the divine a condition of being per se. Those who believe in the divine are not merely believers "on faith" who might otherwise not believe, but they are individuals who recognize the kinship between mortal and divine. Descartes claimed that an argument in favor of God is our so-called clear and distinct notion of God, which supposedly could not exist if God did not exist. Hölderlin's words seem to go a step farther: we can believe in the divine because we ourselves are divine; only our mortality is not always receptive to the idea.

Dilthey pointed out long ago that Hölderlin did not find much comfort in the theology of his day. Kant liberated the young man from the restrictions of theology, with the result that Christ retained value as one mediator of the divine among many.[2] Erich Heller has commented on Hölderlin's more encompassing notion of the divine in relation to Christian tradition; "Hölderlin not only goes outside it, praising and lamenting the gods of ancient Greece, but he places Christ beside them as a bare equal, and in addition—and in this he is at one with many of his contemporaries—looks upon Nature as yet another manifestation of the divine."[3] Though we may never be able to ascertain with absolute certainty where Christ and the God of Christ stand in relation to Hölderlin's greater conception of what is divine, it is at least clear that Christianity is a historical moment of the divine, and one that the poet does not reject. Just as clear, however, is the openness of the poet's thought, since in "Celebration of Peace" the prince of the feast is not Christ, historically the most recent demigod-mediator, but another of unknown identity. Faith as a precondition of poetry is therefore not to be construed as the absolute faith of a Kierkegaard, nor the faith that burns heretics. Hölderlin's use of religiously charged expressions like *faith, god,* and *heaven* provide an immense source of relief to readers who might otherwise be put off by such expressions, as they are all too frequently interpreted in the light of "the faith." But if mankind is to work toward an understanding of itself, its deepest motivations and the limits that we commonly deem "mortal," then Hölderlin's writings on the divine give us an opportunity to rescue from institutional appropriation those universal forms, which seem to have been waiting for centuries.

In something remotely resembling a genesis, Hölderlin speaks of the divinity of nature and the advent of man. "Man" (*Der Mensch*) sets up a relationship between the Father (Helios) and the Mother (Earth), whose most beautiful child is man; when man is not yet of age, he chooses among all fruits the "holy grapevine" as his nurse, and he comes of age. Man resembles neither his father nor his mother but is a hybrid of both in his ups and downs; still, he aspires to be like the mother, who is described as "the mother of gods," the "all-encompassing."[4] Significant in this relatively early poem is the primacy of nature with regard to gods. In the remaining strophes the poet deals with man's self-imposed alienation from his parents as a result of his hybrid genesis, so that man's toil and suffering, his transitoriness, his inability to hold onto peace are indeed hallmarks of mortality, but those that contribute to his unique being, his destiny. The poet concludes:

> Is he not the most blessed of all
> Living things? But deeper and wilder
> Grasps fate, the all balancing one,
> Even the strong man's kindled heart.

The fate that eventually claims man, it will be seen, also claims gods, just as in "Celebration" the law of fate dictates other-knowing. Hölderlin used the personification of nature as mother again in his poem "The Capricious Ones" (*Die Launischen*), this time applied to the poets who are easily reconciled and obedient if only loving nature touches them.[5]

Hölderlin also spoke in terms of a divine genesis in "The Spirit of the Age" (*Der Zeitgeist*), this time addressing himself to the god of time. All around the poet things are becoming too dark, and he appeals to the god of time as to his father, in order to see through the turmoil of his day to the clear source:

> Let me finally, father! meet you with open
> Eyes! did not you first awaken the spirit
> From me with your ray? gloriously
> Bring me to life, o father!—[6]

The allusion to the ray (*Strahl*) waking the life out of the individual reminds us of the poet's role in mediating between gods and men, specifically, in receiving the holy ray that must then be transmitted, harmlessly, to the people ("As on a Holiday"). The poet here attributes the animating ray to the god of time, who is apparently omnipresent insofar as he cannot be escaped and is described in such terms as fate was described in "Man," except that the god of time is said to awaken the souls of youths and impart wisdom to elders as well. Though this god of time bears no particular features beyond the laws of temporality, it is still interesting to note that Hölderlin attributes the animating ray to him; if the poet was brought to life by the sudden event of becoming struck by a ray, perhaps the before-life occurs without the auspices of the god of time who only dispenses time (mortality) when youths "come of age."

In one of his Diotima poems Hölderlin places his beloved in the company of vanished god-men (*Göttermenschen*), who still manifest a company because they are preserved in a continuous lament. Diotima's solitude among mortals is therefore corrected by the more enduring company of immortals, and time itself comes to her aid:

> But time does heal. The heavenly ones are now strong,
>   Are fast. Does not nature once again
>   Take upon itself its ancient, joyous right?[7]

Within time, which here bears the properties attributed to it in "The Capricious Ones," both the heavenly powers and nature are making a come-back. When the poet says that the heavenly ones are strong *now,* he is declaring the primacy of time; the heavenly ones are strong when nature asserts its joyous right. They are both strong and fast in their appearances or manifestations, while at other times, it can be inferred, the heavenly ones are not so strong. Similarly, since nature is reclaiming its right, it must have fallen into obscurity at some interval or another; circumstances must be favorable for the event of the dialogue in time that conjoins gods, mortals, and nature. The preparing, which is central to the poet's vocation, may contribute to a setting in which the dialogue unfolds, but thus far we have seen fate, time, nature, gods, and men as moments of the divine. It would be impossible for the poet to exercise absolute control over the "timing" of the dialogue, insofar as he figures into the lower end of the "power spectrum." When Hölderlin attributes strength and speed to the heavenly ones, we have to ask ourselves: to what end? One possible response indicates the direction of Hölderlin's thoughts on the divine; the heavenly ones and the gods are children of nature and time, and they exercise a will similar to the will of men, which calls them to the celebration of peace, to the site of the communal spirit, just as mortals are summoned.

This focus on the genesis of man intends to provide only a basic groundwork on which to situate a later, more refined analysis of the divine, and for this reason I consulted earlier poems that are not generally considered substantial enough for exploring such a concept. What emerges is the primacy of time and nature, while within this sphere (or spheres) both mortals and gods are perceived as children of nature. Before we leave the genesis idea, however, another look at the final strophe of "Celebration of Peace" will show that Hölderlin trusted his earlier conception of the divine enough to feature it prominently in a great hymn.

> Like the lioness you lamented,
> O mother, as you,
> Nature, lost your children.
> For they were stolen, all too loving one, by
> Your enemy, since you accepted
> Him almost like your own sons,
> And joined gods with satyrs.
> Thus you have built much

And buried much,
For you are hated by that
Which you, all powerful one,
Brought to light before it was time.
Now you know this, and let it be;
For gladly, without feeling lies
Below, until it ripens, the timid busyness.[8]

This conclusion is not exactly in keeping with the celebrative tone of the poem, rather it seems to detach and view the history of men and gods retrospectively from without, as if recounting how we came to the hour of celebration. Nature once again is personified as mother, but now she is a fierce lioness whose young have been taken from her. We know from the earlier context that both mortals and gods are children of nature so that both were taken from her.

What power, we must ask, is capable of driving a wedge between nature and her children, especially since gods are included in the family? The powerful enemy who was at first accepted as a son of nature turns out to have been a mere satyr, that is, a goat-man in comparison to the gods—less than goat (nature), less than man (divine nature). Short of positing the existence of a completely new enemy-god or resurrecting the time-honored "devil" as evil, we can see *man himself* in this *deceptive* and powerful enemy—man, who has many faces and is not always worthy of his gods. "Man" detailed the rise and fall of mankind by showing how man is his own worst enemy, but that is his fate. Nature's enemy is one of its own children, and nature accepts the balance, since she was responsible for prematurely (*vor der Zeit*) giving birth to this enemy, while her other children, of riper temperament, could well be lamented.

Now it is apparent that nature, though described as all-powerful, makes mistakes and laments her losses, but she also waits, that is, "lets be" in the interval of waiting, which points to the relation of nature to time. "Before it was time" (*vor der Zeit*) has two meanings for our purpose, though they cannot fairly emerge in the Hamburger translation, which reads "too soon." *Vor der Zeit* means "prematurely," "before it is time," but it also means "*before time*" in the sense of standing before or in the presence of time. Acting within her powers to bring man into the light, as opposed to letting man ferment below in the darkness, nature is judged by a higher authority than nature, or, let us at least say, is judged according to laws that govern in the realm of nature, mortals, and gods. It could hardly be the fault of nature's gods or mortal children that they are placed in the company of satyrs and become nature's enemy, for she first calls them into being and thereafter lives with the consequences. Nature's motivation is love, and in Hölderlin love occupies an exalted place in the world, not because it is easy, not because it is always smooth and without suffering, but because it exercises a joining effect that brings mortals into the presence of gods and into the presence of nature itself.

The reader of Hölderlin's poetry frequently comes across the notion of the loss of the divine, which early in my study was described as the interval that exists between gods and men. Since we have already established that being as dialogue requires the presence of the divine among mortals, it is certainly more than nostalgia that motivated the poet to lament the loss, or the retreating, of the divine. If the gods are not present, and if there is no possibility for their arrival among men, being itself is threatened, and man cannot come of age. In this sense, both men and gods may continue, in relative stages of other-knowing, even while the divine that encompasses them allows one to retreat momentarily from the other, while the divine per se is not effaced.

In order to understand how the loss of the divine is not absolute in historical terms and how it is regained, let us consider the analogy of the self as being.[9] In the case of self, there is a state of being that is not yet selfhood, but which bears the potential to be self. On this score Nietzsche had a lot to say, and *Zarathustra* is brimming with allusions to the self and positive selfishness, which must be created in the face of adversity represented by the collective—which, for him at least, is the nonself. In very ordinary language, we frequently say of a given action: "I apologize, I was just not myself that day," or some such, which means that, even after achieving selfhood, there are times when it retreats, when it lapses in such a way that an uncharacteristic action may ensue. The communal event of being, in similar fashion, cannot take place without its constituitive elements, so that communal being is not always present. First, it must be established, then, it must be maintained, and here all those factors of other-knowing come into play.

Heidegger also treated the loss of self in his deliberations on *das Man* in *Being and Time*. We have already had occasion to discuss this issue in connection with the everyday use of language as opposed to the language that reveals and calls into being. In Hölderlinian terms, the everyday has the potential to be the holiday, as a special event involving the participation of various dialogic elements, but only if the gods are present in the lives of men. Therefore, just as Hölderlin has intervals of day and night, there are also intervals in the state of being. To speak in terms of the loss of the divine is thus not as damning as one might otherwise assume. It remains to be seen, as precisely as possible, just what is being lost during those intervals when we are not participating in the dialogue and how the dialogue restores the appearance of the divine.

In "Gods Once Wandered . . ." the poet seems to indicate a historically distant time in which the gods, "glorious muses" who heal and inspire, walked among men like the beloved Diotima, who is now the poet's inspiration.[10] Love now sustains the poet, so that in the years to come people would say of their relationship that they lived in a more secret world, known only to the gods. The lovers are known only to the gods, but the relationship is reciprocal; for those who concern themselves only with the mortal will be given over to the earth, while the lovers will be adopted by Aether, having been true to one another and to the gods, whereby they triumph over fate. So even in the absence of the manifestation of gods on earth, they continue to exist and to influence the lives of mortals.

"The Song of the German" can be regarded as an earlier version of "Germania," for the poet shifts his focus from Germany in the present, which is being exploited by others, to the distant past of Minerva's children, whose soul yet lives among men but wanders from land to land.[11] In strophe 8 the poet again names the ray emanating from a god (Zeus), yet this time not as the animating, life-giving ray that calls into being, but as the destructive blast that destroyed Semele and her house. Lamenting the passing of Attica Hölderlin writes:

> O holy wood! o Attica! did He strike
>   Even you with his terrible ray, so soon,
>   And did they who lived within you rush
>   Into the aether, released by flames?

If it is Zeus who is characterized with the pronoun *He* (*Er*), then he did not precipitate a twilight of the gods so much as he brought down his own house in that place designated as the site of communal gathering between gods and men. The "genius" wanders from land to land, and, though the days of Attica's greatness are in the past, Germany's are about to begin.

In a more personal context associated with Diotima, we find the poet unable to participate in any celebration as long as he is paralyzed by the state of godlessness that afflicts him in his separation: "I wish to celebrate, but what? and sing with others, / But in this loneliness I lack anything divine."[12] Celebration and song, as it is undertaken with others, is not possible when the individual feels incapable of anything divine. The relation between being as dialogue and the divine is so close that the disruption of one hinders the other. The poet emerges from his depression only when he presents himself with the image of his beloved, whom he places in the company of the gods as his inspiration. In the final strophe his gratitude and joy have returned, so that the poet thanks the heavenly ones (*ihr Himmlischen*) and is once again capable of

A silence that hinders
the song that does not linger

the "singer's prayer." In fact, the poet has regained his feeling for the divine to such an extent that he cries out in the affirmation of life; he now feels as he once did while standing with Diotima on the sunny heights, and a god speaks to him, animating him, from within the temple.[13] The loss of the divine within the individual poet is therefore signaled by a breakdown in the dialogue, and when the dialogue is reestablished, so that the poet feels the gods within himself and regains his natural gratitude, he is once again "being himself" and expresses it in poetry. Let us turn now to the collective state of being, where a parallel relation exists between being and the divine.

"Bread and Wine" stands as one of the best examples of the dialogue, for it is here that Hölderlin interweaved the destinies of gods and men with subtle balance, culminating in the appearance of Christ the demi-god.

The night encourages the poet's reflection and fills a need of mankind; in our darkness there must be something tenable, and night grants us "forgetting and holy drunkenness," as well as the flowing word. Along with this teleological forgetting the night grants us "holy remembrance" (*Heilig Gedächtniß*) in order to remain awake at night.[14] We observed in "Remembrance" how the sea takes and imparts memory, so that it is not surprising to find Hölderlin using the same device here. The night grants forgetting in order to alleviate the rigors of consciousness and liberate man from the need to establish his own tenable support at all hours, without respite. The holy drunkenness is the healing power, and, while we might assume that this is a state of oblivion, it is mentioned in connection with the flowing word, the sleeplessness and bolder life (*kühneres Leben*), which provides holy remembrance; the "oblivion" is therefore not oblivion but the state of being in which man shares the divine, in which the borders between men and gods are freely crossed. The night has two sides in this poem; as respite from the brightness and toil of the day, it pulls us into the proximity of the holy by virtue of letting us forget. But this forgetting enables us to find something to hold onto, that is its holiness in the face of the day's resistance, which amounts, it seems, to the same thing as darkness. By day we are not always being, as earlier we observed that being comes and goes, so that a deeper stratum of being is accessed by the advent of forgetting. The greater night is holy recollecting, which, in turn, enables us to remain awake (being) at night. This meaning of night was indicated by Hölderlin in "The Poet's Vocation," where Dionysos awakens the peoples from sleep.

The being that night enables is very carefully described in strophe 3, where a unique freedom to traverse the whole extent of being serves to place us directly in the company of gods, through the event of recollecting through poetry.

> Divine fire also drives us, by day and by night,
> To move on. So come! that we may look upon the open,
>   That we may seek what is proper, distant as it may be.
> One thing remains firm; be it midday or going on
>   Into midnight, always a measure exists,
> Common to all, yet also to each is granted a proper share,
> Each goes and comes to the place where he can.[15]

We are called into being by divine fire, or by the presence of the gods who call us. In ontological terms, it makes no difference whether the gods call us or we summon them, for the dialogue is what counts, and that dialogue of being requires both mortals and gods. Man is therefore on the threshold of being when the dialogue ensues, and being encourages movement within a measure. Being is the occupying of its own proper space, but this proper-ty (*ein Eigenes, eignes*) must be explored. The poet's exhortation to come and look upon the open (*das Offene schauen*), and to seek there what is proper or one's own, is an invitation to come into one's own, to come into being. The measure that is common to all while rendering to individuals what is properly theirs is the law that governs beings; *das Eigene* is what is proper to each being, and no other being can appropriate what measure has not given to it. In this sense Hölderlin warned in "The Rhine" that, even though the gods need mortals in order to experience emotion, we must never aspire to be gods, as their proper being is given them by measure.

In strophes 3–6 Hölderlin re-presents himself with the ancients of Greece, and he summons us to move on to that place because "From that place and back to it points the coming god."[16] We can assume that the identity of this "coming god" is revealed in the final strophe as Christ, the "torch-bearer," but, historically speaking, Christ has already arrived, even though Hölderlin chose to speak in the present tense as though the event were only now unfolding. The union of past and present is understandable enough as the event of dialogue, insofar as mortals and gods are joined in dialogue, but could this coming god be the unidentified prince of the feast? It would not be too much to say that at least the coming god represents the same spirit as the prince of the feast, since Christ is in attendance there but is not the indicated guest.

The seventh strophe of "Bread and Wine" has given commentators much to remark upon. Having provided a history of how mortals interact with their gods, the poet returns to the present and is not at all pleased with the status quo; mortals no longer bear the marks of their gods on their foreheads, and gods no longer traffic among mortals in mortal form. Hence the poet writes: "But friend! we arrive too late. The gods live, yes, / But over our heads beyond in another world." There is a natural, or organic, quality to man's relation to the divine, such that, without the dialogue, being is reduced to mere existence, to filling the interval with distractions that do not contribute to one's discovery of the proper. In "Menon's Lament" we observed how the poet could not celebrate, though he wanted to, because he was without any feeling of the divine's presence. This same theme is sounded in strophe 7 of "Bread and Wine," where the poet asks "wherefore poets in paltry times?" The paltry times (in dürftiger Zeit) are now a matter of concern for everyone, not only the poet lamenting his separation from the beloved, and the paltry times must yield to a climate more favorable for song and collective celebration before mankind can expect to once again enjoy the presence of the gods. The gods are not dead; they are temporarily out of reach. Hölderlin expresses hope for the renewal of being as dialogue by using the symbols of bread and wine, the earth and the gift of the gods, as the living promise that can again be filled.

The gods who "were otherwise here" (strophe 8) will return at the proper time, and for this reason the poets sing of the wine-god and offer praise. This poetry is "not idly conceived" as the poet insists, meaning that poetry as a function of preparing for the appearance of the gods is more than the term aesthetic could exhaust. Dionysos, as the reconciler of day and night, is the communal god who bridges light and darkness in the interval of being because among gods his role is to intervene in behalf of mortals. The original intervention was the awakening with holy wine, but being continues whenever Dionysos is called upon by the poet to join all mortals with their gods. This theme is continued in the final strophe when Hölderlin says that we are the living prophecy expressed in ancient song, the children of god, but we remain heartless, "shadows," until Father Aether is known by everyone and belongs to everyone (erkannt jeden und allen gehört).

The Greeks with their gods represent one chapter in the history of the dialogue, while with Christ another chapter begins. In any case, Christ continues in the function of Dionysos for he is described as the son of the highest, bearing a torch, bringing his light even among the shadows. There is no jealousy on the part of the Greek gods; Christ's appearance among men is welcomed by the wise, by the titan, and even the envious Cerberus is at peace. In this final strophe we have both Dionysos and Christ, both Father Aether and God. Two divine expressions of the highest share with mankind by placing one of their own kind among us. In order for the dialogue to be a true measure of being, everyone must know Father Aether, and he must belong to all; the reciprocal element of the dialogue is clear, for, in order to participate, mortals must constitute a community based on authority not found among mortals alone.

We have studied the question of the loss, or retreating, of the divine and learned how the gods do not always appear but are otherwise accessible within Hölderlin's broader conception of the divine. The regaining of the divine depends on conditions that Hölderlin mentions in many of his poems; there must be a preparing for the gods, preserving of their memory through lore, an awakening to the presence of the divine, mediating between divine and mortal, and there must be the possibility for communal being, not only among mortals, but between mortals and gods. All of these preconditions are addressed by the poet, but, as I cautioned near the beginning of this discussion, *the poet does not ordain the timing* of all of this. Time is the dimension in which gods and mortals work, and Hölderlin claimed that nature called man into being prematurely, which indicates that laws higher than those established by men and gods govern throughout Hölderlin's notion of the divine.

So as not to belabor this issue, I have selected two prominent poems in which the loss and regaining of the divine are discussed, but from the standpoint of the proper time. "Nature and Art, or Saturn and Jupiter" treats the injustice of Saturn's banishment to the underworld at the hands of his son, Jupiter. What Jupiter has done was in violation of the laws of time, for, though he now "rules high by day" and enjoys the exercise of power, of giving laws in his ruler arts, the poets recall how the holy father was forced into the underworld, though he was without guilt and though his reign was characterized as the golden age in which his greatness was manifested without having to voice commands.[17] During the golden age, mortals did not even call on Saturn by name, such was his greatness.

The identification of Jupiter with the daytime, and with laws, power, fame and the ruling arts, is the mark of his more "modern" character as a god, but it is also a mark of his premature rise to power. The poet will not recognize Jupiter until he in turn recognizes Saturn, who was after all before him as a natural ancestor. The powers enjoyed by Jupiter have their origins in the peace of Saturn, and Jupiter must allow that the poets name Saturn, who hitherto remained unnamed.

As opposed to the artistry and busyness of the daytime represented by Jupiter, the poet makes his acceptance of the later god conditional upon first experiencing "what is alive" and upon regaining the bliss of Saturn's reign by overcoming "the changing time." Having dwelled for a time in the atmosphere of Saturn's age, and having proven to himself that the world of Saturn is every bit as alive and praiseworthy as Jupiter's, the poet is now ready to accept Jupiter-Kronion (son of Saturn, that is, of Chronos) and to hear him, for now Jupiter and men are like the son of time, both making laws and "proclaiming what holy twilight conceals."

Jupiter's laws and his expression of what holy twilight conceals have meaning to the poet only if they are in their proper context, that is, only if they rest on a real authority and are not simply functions that Jupiter has usurped. In order for Jupiter to be heard by men and to participate in the dialogue, things must first be taken care of in his family and within his community of gods—all beings are subject to the laws of time. The giving of laws is a central concept in the poem; Jupiter does it, quite secure in his ruler arts, and mortals do it. But what does it mean within the context of nature? Before Jupiter there are no laws, yet there is peace. The laws of day, that time in which everything appears to be clear only because it is by decree that things fall into place, is a law in violation of time. Law assumes communal meaning and therefore loses its arbitrary or artful character only when the balance has been restored between nature and art, between Saturn and Jupiter. This requires a proper perspective of time on the part of both men and gods or a proper relation to the divine, which governs all being. This proper relation is the dialogue that the poet, on behalf of his community, agrees to join, and once again the dialogue involves men and gods because *both* proclaim, and have equal right to proclaim, what is not of the day—namely, holy twilight.

The final strophes of "Germania" pursue the theme of the proper time for the return of the gods. The time for Germania's silence is now past, according to the poet, and she must assume her proper place within the community of peoples, for the gods have chosen her as the site of the dialogue. Germania is poised in the middle of time; in her waters and in the storms of her forests "sounds forth from ancient times the divine past," but the poet exclaims: "How different it is!"[18] Germania's location in the present makes these manifestations of the divine past relevant, alive, and in the same breath the poet describes how the future speaks joyfully out of the distance. Germania, however, is situated in the middle of time, between past and future (*Doch in der Mitte der Zeit*), and Hölderlin strengthens this expression of being at the right time by relating how Germania lives peacefully with the virgin earth and with the ether, whom we recognize as Father Aether in "Bread and Wine." Until Father Aether is known by all, and is embraced by everyone, there can be no communal spirit governing over a community within which the dialogue may unfold. "Germania" brings us into that community, and, poised in the middle of time, with her proper relation to the divine past and future, Germania's holidays serve to unite gods and mortals, while she serves as priestess among the peoples.

In "The Rhine" Hölderlin used the great river as a metaphor for the fate of man; just as it originates gloriously in the mountains of Switzerland but later on learns its proper measure by quietly filling the German countryside with agriculture and cities, so, too, man must come to realize his proper place in the world, particularly in relation to the gods. For man is prone to question authority, as we read in strophe 7, by distorting the bonds of love into chains, and he will frequently choose to despise the fate of mortals and aspire to be like the gods. We saw Hölderlin's treatment of this theme in "Celebration of Peace," where man was brought into the light by nature before it was time, and also in "Man," where men aspire to be like nature, who is mother of gods and men. But in "The Rhine" the poet offers a glimpse of just how close mortals and gods are, or, perhaps, how related they are, in spite of the limitations given to each.

The poet explains that, while the gods or heavenly ones are generally satisfied with immortality, still they lack one thing; since they cannot feel, the gods require mortals to feel in their behalf.[19] In the poet's role in manifesting life, man is given greater vitality in this sharing relationship, just as Hölderlin related on numerous occasions that he felt animated by the gods when his natural state of being was restored, but he felt dead without it. The gods, too, benefit from this relationship, since their being would be without sensation if not for the nearness of man. This reciprocity must not be misjudged, however, and Hölderlin cautions that mortals must accept the difference and not desire to be like the gods. Given the existence of this mutually rewarding balance, the poet indicates in strophe 13 that men and gods can celebrate a wedding feast, "All the living celebrate, / And balanced / For a while is fate."[20] This balancing of fate is extremely important, as it occurs only when men and gods are in their proper time and in their proper relation to one another. Normally, fate would rule in such a way that one or the other, usually man, would "be out of time," thereby requiring fate to impose upon him the limitations of his being.

The limitations of the gods are once again addressed in "Mnemosyne" and in such a way as to demonstrate the partial reliance of the gods upon mortals, but the poem is extremely difficult, and scholars do not agree on which version to present as the final one. Beissner, of course, gives all three versions, and his notes (GSA 2, 2, 824–30) are very helpful, while Hamburger offers the third version, which does not keep the centrally important first strophe. Sieburth, on the other hand, uses the second version and indicates that it may have been written as late as 1805, therefore during the period of Hölderlin's worsening psychic condition.[21] I will use the second version as it is given by Sieburth.

Mnemosyne was the Greek goddess of memory, the titan daughter of Uranus, who personifies heaven, and Gaea, personifying earth. Given this parentage in the mythology and Hölderlin's illumination of remembrance as a function of poetry that establishes the dialogue, we can expect the poem to contain elements common to several of the major poems. The first strophe begins with a suggestion of man's failure within the measure of his being, because the poet points from the outset to language:

> A sign are we, meaningless
> Painless are we and have nearly
> Lost our language in foreign lands.[22]

For us language is not merely speech, but dialogue, and to have nearly lost our language in foreign places suggests that man is not how/where he properly is. It is helpful at this point also to recollect that in "Bread and Wine" divine fire drives us to move on, to look upon the open, and to seek what is proper; here, however, man seems to have wandered into an oblivion where language no longer expresses being. In this sense an observation by Sieburth concerning the meaning of the sign in "Mnemosyne," "Patmos," and ". . . The Vatican . . ." sheds light on the opening lines:

> But the enigma of the sign lies not merely in language's capacity to mean, or to refer, or to signify, but, more crucially, in the mysterious fact that language (and hence man) can *be* at all—. . . . As an activity of *naming,* poetry does not so much imitate or represent or symbolize something beyond or prior to itself, but simply *says,* and, in so doing, establishes a site where what is said is all that lasts.[23]

Sieburth's remark brings out the essential link between language and being while offering us another clue about how language might become lost. The closing line of "Remembrance" reads: "What endures, though, the poets ordain."[24]

Another clarification of the opening lines of "Mnemosyne" is Stanley Corngold's; he points out that the poet not only establishes a site as a function of the poet's service but also asserts himself: "The assertion of the near loss of language and the advancing logic of the poem show the poet engaged in a movement toward recollection, toward self-assurance, for the sake of commemoration but also for his own sake as a being who names and is not merely a name."[25] Like "Remembrance," "Mnemosyne" points to the one who remembers in the sense of actively recollecting, for this activity brings together the poet's own, his *proprium.*

From the language of man Hölderlin moves on to the language of nature, or the divine. These two are directly related, however, for there is a quarrel in the heavens concerning man, such that the moons race violently (*gewaltig / Die Monde gehn*), while the sea speaks, and streams must find their course. The speeding of the moons indicates imbalance, and, even while the sea, home of the rivers, speaks, the river must find its own way, indicating a break in the dialogue of being that involves mortals and gods. In spite of this turmoil, Hölderlin writes

> doubtless
> However is One. He
> Can change this any day. Scarcely does he need
> Law.

This One who *is* without doubt is seemingly untouched by the quarrel or the loss of speech, and he is so great as to almost defy law. Hölderlin completes this line with the following enigmatic words: "And the page sounds and oak trees sway then next / To the glaciers."[26] This One who is capable of restoring order knows how to reconcile mortal with immortal, for when the poets write, the divine is also present, and mortals are lifted to their proper heights as well, just as the oaks now thrive where they otherwise could not grow, near the glaciers. The whole problem of language failing and, along with it, being fading, is lucidly explained in the lines that follow and conclude the first strophe:

> For the heavenly ones
> Are not capable of everything. Indeed, sooner
> Would mortals reach the abyss. Hence the echo turns
> With them. Long is
> Time, but the true
> Will happen.

The German for "happen" in this case is *sich ereignen,* which is related to seeing something and becoming visible, manifest. The happening of the true, or what is true, is the event celebrated by Hölderlin in numerous poems, namely, the meeting of gods and mortals within the proper place, at the proper time.

The last lines of the first strophe require careful scrutiny, as Hölderlin's conception of the divine displays its mortal character here. The heavenly ones, or the gods, are not omnipotent, and their very plurality as gods makes them accountable to the same laws that govern in time for all beings. Mortals would sooner reach the abyss, says Hölderlin, than these gods, but why? Again we are confronted with the question of how gods must rely on mortals, and the meaning of the abyss must open up here. A solid treatise could be written on the abyss in Hölderlin's conception, and literature already exists that address this issue, but, as the issue is now at hand, let it suffice to say that the abyss is the furthest extent of being, the point at which being no longer is. In terms of time, the abyss is as far away from the site of man's being as is the moment of perfect clarity toward which man strives. To say, therefore, that

Abyss

mortals are closer to the abyss is not to fault them for being lowly, or for becoming dragged down; this reading is countered by the image of the echo turning with mortals. The sound that is produced and sent out into the abyss like a probe is produced by man in his efforts to explore being, to find his proper place. The sound echoes off man, as he is the more substantial "surface" within the enormous interval between pinnacle and abyss. This interval, as time, is of course long, but, in spite of time's expanse, the true will come into its own.

So often in Hölderlin's poetry one finds the juxtaposition of being with the divine as opposed to merely existing without song, without celebration or cause for celebration. In "Germania" the site of being is established, and Germany is situated in the middle of time. In "Nature and Art," a proper balance must be observed by both gods and men in order to establish being in the present on a genuine footing. Man's efforts to establish being in the proper place and time are embodied in poetry because language is the medium in common of all beings. This poetic language of being, however, expresses the total of all man's striving, all work of men, as that which the gods themselves do not perform. The gods do not even feel, and for this they require mortals. Their appearing and disappearing remains linked to the care with which mortals attend to the dialogue, as can be seen when the entire first strophe of "Mnemosyne" is viewed as a context similar to strophe 3 of "Bread and Wine."

Divine fire drives or urges man "to move on." Being is not static, in the sense that mortals must look upon the open and seek what is proper, and, though a measure rules always and for everyone, to each is given his own.[27] This enterprising aspect of being, not controlled by mortals but characteristic of man as long as holy remembrance is present, is what Hölderlin alludes to in "Mnemosyne." Man has almost lost language in foreign places, that is, in gazing upon the open and moving on to find his proper place. He would sooner reach the abyss because it is given to him to go out searching, but this search is a long one, and not always is man capable of observing the proper balance between the past and the future. Instrumental in the overcoming of strife and the reconciliation of poetry with nature is the One who is so conspicuously situated above gods and mortals. Since the echo turns with mortals and the true will happen in spite of the greatness of time, the appearance of the One and the true both seem to hinge on man's efforts.

Hölderlin continues to interweave mortal and divine in the second and third strophes.[28] This middle strophe, however, takes place in the present and is compacted into one great image. The poet opens the meditation by addressing someone: "But how, loved one?" "We" next see some familiar and everyday sights: dust on the ground, the shadows of the woods, smoke trailing above the rooftops and among the city's turrets. This peaceful setting prompts the poet to observe:

> good namely are
> The signs of day, when a heavenly one
> Has wounded the soul with contradiction.

The strife depicted in strophe one, with gods quarreling over mortals, is dispelled by the simplicity and peacefulness of the mortal's day. From this cityscape the poet moves on to a broader, symbolic image in the high Alpine mountains. I agree with Beissner that the image is significant in showing the balance of time that resides in the present, similar to Germania's situation in the middle of time poised between the past and the future ("Germania," last strophe.).[29]

Hölderlin describes the snow, which is half gone, high in the mountains; like the lilies of May, it gleams among the burgeoning greenery, giving testimony of what is noble. And in this high pass (*auf hoher Straß*) a wanderer is walking, "speaking of the cross," which has been placed along the way in honor of the dead.

> in the high pass
> A wanderer walks angrily
> With the other,
> Distantly intuiting, but what is this?

Beissner sheds light on these lines by explaining that in periods of transition the divine reveals itself in anger, as in "Patmos" (strophe 12).[30] The wanderer is the mortal who intuits the distant other, namely the divine, and is accompanied by the other because he, as mortal, is speaking of the cross. This cross, reminding us of the departed, situated as it is high in the mountain pass, is the symbol of transition, and another sign of remembrance. It indicates the past and those who walked this way before, bringing into this image of the present the presence of the divine and the future.

In the third and final strophe Hölderlin personalizes the death of his heroes: "By the fig tree did my / Achilles die." In addition to Achilles, Ajax and Patroclus are named, "And there died / Still many others." But not only mortals perished and are remembered, for Mnemosyne, too, was marked for death by having a lock of her hair removed as "god laid down his cloak." The cutting of a lock signified death, and God's setting aside his cloak signifies the closing of the age of the gods and the coming of night.[31] The closing lines of the poem are:

> The heavenly ones namely are
> Indignant, when one has not gathered in his soul,
> Caringly, but yet he must; like him
> Mourning also errs.

The mortal who would sacrifice his soul is the one who recognizes no measure, who refuses to observe the laws of being as they are given to gods and, differently, to men. Beissner does well to point out the eighth strophe of "The Rhine" in this context, for there we have already seen that mortals must not aspire to share in the existence of gods. Mourning would have no place in the event that man squandered his being.

"Mnemosyne" is a poem in which the poet himself alternates between the dimensions of time. In the first strophe we learn of the danger of losing our language and of a quarrel in the heavens over man. From this initial moment of imbalance, however, the poet revealed the One who reconciles, and voiced his confidence in man, who has it within his power to achieve being and manifest the true. The last strophe is less promising, and it dwells among the dead; the brightest note is perhaps the cautionary note contained in the last sentence and, certainly, the naming of Mnemosyne, who is memory itself. The middle strophe, on the other hand, also functions as the middle ground, the balance, and it takes place in the present with man depicted as a wanderer, on his way. But even the image of the solitary wanderer is not without mention of the dialogue alive in man's heart, and past and future converge in man the individual, and man the inhabitant of cities.

The dispensational element of being is that before which man is powerless, but this condition is not to be lamented, for in Hölderlin even gods and nature are subject to the law of fate, the laws of time. And though man is situated on a different level of being than are gods, still, man is the more enterprising, more promising one, whose work and struggle join all beings together and provide a context for other-knowing, for celebration, for the communal spirit, for dialogue. Perhaps the dispensational element of being is less "divine" than it is natural, or, in any case, it is divine only insofar as man is himself the willing agent of divinity and its best expression. As opposed to something posited beyond the grasp of man, as a thing in itself that will never be revealed, or that will be revealed in time only to the "initiated," Hölderlin's conception of the divine requires mortal agency and is consummated only among mortals. Indeed, the divine might be nothing other than nature itself, as the poet insists in his preface to "Celebration of Peace" that in speaking as he did, he "could not do otherwise." On a beautiful day, he continued, almost every manner of song can be heard, "and nature, from which it springs, also takes it back again." The possibility of poetry, as an act of joining in celebra-tion and manifesting being, owes much to nature. Surely Hölderlin, who had more to say concerning nature than most, would have had sufficient reason to place nature and the divine on a more or less equal footing, and to pull them both together in man.

10

Shipping Out

Columbus and the Voyage of Discovery

Throughout this study Nietzsche has been cited wherever a comparison between his conception of being and Hölderlin's sheds light on what is the proper activity of man. This relationship is a deliberate one because Hölderlin and Nietzsche held similar positions in their critique of the modern personality, but also because there is a major difference between the thinkers once the question of alternative is raised. In the most glaring sense, Nietzsche the "antipoet," the "antiromantic" rejects the claim of poetry to instruct us about man, while Hölderlin embraces poetry as precisely that medium through which man comes into his own. The juxtaposition of Hölderlin with Nietzsche is valid not only within the theoretical framework of what poetry is, but more so as a continuation of the critique of romanticism launched by Nietzsche; in putting distance between himself and the romanticists, whom he considered to be passively nihilistic and idealistic, Nietzsche was attempting to escape the reach of metaphysics.

In our examination of Hölderlin's unusual conception of the divine, with its strict reliance on performance in the here and now as its criterion of authenticity, I emphasized that Nietzsche lays stress on the creative will, but that he admonishes us not to create what is beyond the strength of man to realize. There is in Nietzsche an activity that is "proper" to man, one that does not undermine itself nihilistically, and this activity (for lack of a better word) resides in the dynamic process set in play where man divests himself of what is borrowed in order to recreate himself on the strength of what he has earned, experienced in the trial of "living dangerously." In Nietzsche's thought the enemies, frequently personified, are inertia and gravity, sleep and complacency, closed-ness and security. The restlessness of the human spirit is personified in grand style, indeed archetypally, in the wandering prophet

Zarathustra, who is himself engaged in the activity of creating the self while exhorting his listeners to follow suit (though not to follow him). *Thus Spoke Zarathustra* is the poetic expression of that activity that we now call *Lebensphilosophie,* or the philosophy of life. For the moment let us consider Zarathustra in his role as the wanderer, the one who does not rest, stop, or advocate any specific activity except the one in which all being should be engaged, namely the activity of finding man.

In Hölderlin, too, the moving on is a truly vital pursuit. This is not to say that Hölderlin used semantically charged ciphers such as "live dangerously!" or "self-overcoming," for these are already markers of the age of existentialism or, in any case, markers of an age in which the absence or nonpresence of God figures prominently in the reflections of philosophers. Again, Hölderlin does not prescribe the same destination, say, as does Nietzsche with the exhortation to move on; it is the moving on in and of itself that deserves our immediate attention. Once again, consider the third strophe of "Bread and Wine."

> Divine fire also drives us, by day and by night,
> To move on. So come! that we may look upon the open,
> That we may seek what is proper, distant as it may be.
> One thing remains firm; be it midday or going on
> Into midnight, always a measure exists,
> Common to all, yet also to each is granted a proper share,
> Each goes and comes to the place where he can.[1]

What I have rendered as "what is proper" is *ein Eigenes,* and no moral dimension should be attached to "proper." Rather *proper* in the sense of property as derived from *proprius* serves perfectly.

We are driven to move on by day and by night, always driven, and the divine fire, or soul, is what drives us. If Nietzsche's Zarathustra is not driven by the divine, let us at least admit that, frequently, Zarathustra engages in a monologue with his soul, or personified "life"; wisdom and additional "others" stand in close relation to him. The moving on is called for because, in Hölderlin's speech, there is not only an "out there" that the adventurer might traverse, but *the open,* which is a clearing, an opportunity to explore and to locate what is proper. As the poet clearly says, what is certain is the measure that exists common to all and *to each one.* "Each goes and comes to the place where he can" is an expression of destiny, an expression of possibility of fulfilling what is proper to one, again not in a moral sense, but ontically ("where he *can*").[2]

Since Hölderlin and Nietzsche had observations to make on the nature of moving on, both as a movement from the source and an exploration of the open, we want to get at what is proper by comparing, where appropriate, but by distinguishing always. It is most helpful to focus on texts in which the themata of moving on are clearly present, and in this case there are two distinct lyrical expressions, namely the Columbus poems of Hölderlin and Nietzsche. But let us begin with an understanding: that what is of Hölderlin will remain Hölderlin, and what is of Nietzsche will remain Nietzsche. Furthermore, we should hold to the theme of "one's own" as that which describes what one is and how one comes into one's own perhaps in the spirit of Nietzsche's subtitle to *Ecce homo:* "How one becomes what one is."

Nietzsche made himself very clear on the subject of Hölderlin and did not see much affinity between himself and the favorite poet of his adolesence; by the time Nietzsche found his own bearings, he had dismissed several mentors and spiritual companions, and, unfortunately, Hölderlin was one. For the "strong" Nietzsche, the man who had overcome his own idealism and romanticism, Hölderlin was just another weakling who could not survive the climate of Goethe's day; he was another Kleist or Leopardi, and Nietzsche became able to "laugh about his ruin."[3] We have a right to question whether Nietzsche actually understood Hölderlin or took the time to seriously consider his writings. Hölderlin was the poet whose philosophy emerges naturally from the poetry, whereas, in Nietzsche's case, the earliest inclinations were toward rather traditional lyrics that he had to excise, so that Nietzsche remade himself in the mold of the philosopher.

Heidegger has written: "'Nietzsche and Hölderlin'—an abyss separates both. In an abysmally different way both determine the nearest and the furthest future of the Germans and of the West."[4] We do well to heed this warning. Perhaps the abyss that separates Hölderlin and Nietzsche is the primary reason why Nietzsche never found time for a protracted study of the poet beyond what he did as a pupil at *Schulpforta*. Nietzsche had spent such energy on Kant, Goethe, Schopenhauer, Wagner, and the Greeks. When he rejected all others, however, he retained his love for the Greeks and would have had at least this in common with Hölderlin. But as Friedrich Schlegel wrote in connection with the study of the ancients, "each person has found in the ancients what he needed or wished, preferably himself."[5]

This analysis cannot explore the abyss indicated by Heidegger, though his commentaries are frequently useful. In the spirit of "to each his own" and not in the spirit of closing or disguising the abyss, the issue of shipping out will be examined in the light of the Columbus poems. What is at stake here is the discovery of the New World, and the poetic treatment of sea travel in the exploration of man's place in the world. Man's relation to the sea figures prominently in this discussion, though Hölderlin's treatment of the great rivers in such poems as "The Rhine" add considerably. In order to keep a focus on the *proprium* (*das Eigene, ein Eigenes*) of man, Columbus and his activity as the seafarer—this specific heroic type as depicted by Hölderlin and Nietzsche—should give us the substantial mass from which to restructure two intriguing worldviews.

Nietzsche mentioned Columbus in the meditation *On the Use and Disadvantage of History for Life*, but only to indicate that Columbus's discovery of the New World ranked in his mind as one of history's greatest moments.[6] Similarly, Columbus is mentioned in *The Dawn*.[7] It is hereafter, though, that the historical figure becomes a cipher for Nietzsche's own experience and a major tenet of the philosophy of life. He spent three consecutive winters in Genoa, beginning in 1880, and parts of 1883. When Nietzsche embarked on the journey that would bring him into contact with Lou Salomé, he had shipped out of Genoa to Messina on a Sicilian freighter, and from Messina he was invited to Rome, where Paul Rée and Lou had been staying with Malwida von Meysenbug.[8] Though Nietzsche later spoke fondly of the Genoa winters, they were not entirely happy. He was alone there, as he usually was during the decade of his greatest work, and he developed a relationship with the sea. This inner or spiritual relationship could be compared with Genoa's position as a seaport; it was the point of embarkation, but at the same time it represented home and safety, while beyond lay danger and the unknown. The isolation that Nietzsche experienced while in Genoa was a combination of his longing to fulfill missions of exploration and his real homelessness; even in Genoa, home for sailors and explorers, he was not at home. It is during this period that we begin to find him using the Genoa relationship to his creative advantage. His texts begin to reflect how the experience of waiting, looking out upon the sea, enduring solitude, and generally shunning comfort become symbolic of seeking out one's own. We should bear in mind that "one's own" here is strictly and closely Nietzsche's own, in the sense that his philosophizing is the journal of his activity.

One's own is what stands in juxtaposition to everyone else's. One's own is the authentic, experienced, forged in the trials of living, while the other's is safely and painlessly derived from the herd. In Nietzsche's case the others do not hold the same attraction and devotion seen in Hölderlin for reasons that will become clear. In *The Gay Science* there is an aphorism entitled "To the Ships!" The discussion begins with the idea of how a complete philosophical justification of the individual's manner of living and thinking is able to suspend or neutralize the negative criticism rendered by society or one's inner monologue, the conscience. This style of independence is compared to the warming sun, and Nietzsche makes a plea for many such suns to be created. "Even the evil one, the unhappy one, even the exceptional person should have his philosophy, his right, his sunshine!" The last thing such an individual needs, however, is pity. For the exceptional person to become the object of pity, he also becomes "wrong" by virtue of his exceptionality, and the collective renders him neutral by expending pity and its implied condemnation. Pity is not the answer for such types, "rather a new *justice* is needed! And a new game plan! And new philosophers! Even the moral earth is round! Even the moral earth has its antipodes! Even the antipodes have their right to existence! There is still another world to discover—and more than one! To the ships, you philosophers!"[9] The idea of discovering new worlds of morality, as Columbus had brought fresh air to the Old World, expresses Nietzsche's growing sense of what is required to actually grow and stand on one's own. Just as it had earlier been thought that the earth was flat, and that to travel too far in any direction would be to fall off or to encounter sea monsters in the abyss, so, too, has European man regarded his morality as something inescapable, cast in stone, an absolute system with no room for the exceptional, no room for what Nietzsche understood as the natural man, since for him morality is antinature. His exhortation to board the ships is the symbolic expression of embarking, of leaving the safe harbor, in order to experience life beyond the herd, to discover the New World of the self, which will have its own warming sun. Nietzsche's exhortations are brimming with enthusiasm, and his appeal to step into the open, even if one should have to create one's own sun in order to endure the chill of the open, indicates his view that man does not stand before the void but before the expanse that shall become animated by man.

The above thought from the fourth book of *Gay Science,* "Sanctus Januarius," was completed in January 1882. The fourth book has a dedication in rhyme to the spirit of January that begins:

> You who with your spear of flame
> Split the ice upon my soul,
> That it rushes out to sea
> Speeding toward its highest hope . . .[10]

This is a very upbeat, playful lyric, but its importance should not be dismissed. Nietzsche spent the winters in Genoa for the same reason he spent them in other warm, southern climates—he was looking for dry weather and sun, as it was a question of health. When the ice that had encrusted his soul is pierced by January's spear, the soul is liberated; it rushes out to sea, storms forth, indicating that the thaw, or good weather, is not welcomed in order to enjoy momentary comfort but as good sailing weather, favorable winds for exploration. It is out on the open seas that Nietzsche will realize his highest hope. In *Ecce homo,* where he discussed *The Dawn: Thoughts on Moral Prejudice,* he stated: "With this book begins my campaign against *morality.*"[11]

Observe how the sun, or the many suns, are rising suns in keeping with the proverb from the *Rigveda,* which Nietzsche attached to the title page of *Dawn,* while in *Gay Science* the old morality, that is, *the* morality is under attack. This is the meaning of being at sea.

Not surprisingly, Nietzsche also alluded here to his Genoa experience; in spite of the serious and iconoclastic agenda of *Dawn,* the reader, he claimed, will notice no overt malice, no violence, no mean-spirited negativity. Instead, the book and he himself are compared to a sea animal sunning itself on the coastal rocks: "Ultimately I myself was this sea animal: almost every sentence of the book was conceived, *captured* in that maze of rocks near Genoa, where I was alone and still had secrets with the sea."[12] Where the jagged land meets the sea in a maze of rock, this land, which is neither properly the sea nor land, uninhabitable for man, Nietzsche lay sunning himself like a sea animal; in this case the nameless sea animal corresponds to its own sun, its own warmth. A similar analogy was used in the foreword to *Human, All Too Human,* where Nietzsche discussed his convalescence in terms of the lizard that patiently suns itself (sec. 5). Once again the context is the same: illness, solitude, patience, and the eventual triumph, the creative work, which is the reason why one comes home to port, namely, to come into one's own. In *Ecce* he wrote nostalgically of the Genoa period, grateful that it had given him so much. The secrets that he shared with the sea during that trying period were his first authentic lessons, his first initiation into seafaring; henceforth, exploration of the New World as the new "rounded earth" of moral possibilities would be an established symbol, called upon frequently to define, and to celebrate, the enterprising human spirit that embraces the sea.

Even after the Genoa sojourns Nietzsche continued to relate the experience of solitude with the seafaring spirit of Columbus, as seen in his letter of 22 February 1884 to Rohde; ". . . everything is *gone,* the past, comfort; people still see each other, and talk, in order to break the silence. . . . Meanwhile I go my own way, actually it is a journey, a sea journey—and I did not live many years in the city of Columbus for nothing."[13] The *Zarathustra* years did not bring Nietzsche his recognition, and they did not bring him any closer to his friends either. In fact, the sacrifices he continued to make during the writing of *Zarathustra* only increased his isolation and forced him further out to sea. A fragment not used in that work reads: "At sea. 'Blow wind.' *Columbian.* Premonitions, driving forces, where to? / Irrevocably sacrificed. The wanderer. Late autumn."[14] Written just a few months before the letter to Rohde, the fragment reveals how not only Nietzsche, but also the alter ego Zarathustra, are driven about on the sea; the element of sacrifice is evident, as though the seafaring individual leaves not only his home behind, which is *terra firma* in every sense of the word, but also all sources of consolation.

In part 3 of *Zarathustra* Nietzsche begins with a sea voyage that takes Zarathustra away from his friends. Reflecting on his many wanderings across rough terrain, Zarathustra speaks to himself: "Whence do the highest mountains come? so I once asked. Then I learned, that they come from the sea. . . . From the deepest the highest must rise to its height."[15] This may be seen as a parable of individual development, for one must first plumb the depths and negotiate the wilderness of the sea before one can rise into one's own. It is significant, too, that Zarathustra relates his "Vision and Riddle" to sailors who are his companions on the sea voyage. Though at first he merely listens in silence, eventually, "the ice of his heart melts," and he relates the tale of the dwarf, the shepherd, and the snake. But first he explains why the sailors are precisely the ones who should hear his tale:

> You, the bold seekers, attempters, and whoever set
> sail upon terrible seas with cunning sails—
> you, the riddle-drunken, twilight-gladdened ones,
> whose soul is lured to every labyrinth by flutes:
> —for you do not wish to feel your way along a thread
> with cowardly hands; and where you are able to *guess,*
> there you hate to *infer*—[16]

Only because they are friends of danger who will negotiate the labyrinth without Ariadne's thread to guide them, who will come into their own by their own means and under their own power, are the sailors able to receive the most important parable of Zarathustra. For just as the dwarf only comes to Zarathustra's height because he has been a parasitic passenger on his shoulder, those who are not capable of taking their own journey and arriving at their own conclusions are likewise inauthentic, without self.

The fourth part of *Zarathustra* also begins with sea imagery whose symbolic importance must not be overlooked. "The Honey Sacrifice" relates how Zarathustra wants honey to sacrifice, or actually to lure, his elusive catch—namely, man. The world is described as both a jungle and, more so, "an abysmal wealthy sea. . . . Open up and toss me your fish and glittering crabs! With my best bait I lure today the most wondrous men-fish!"[17] The question of Zarathustra's catch was discussed elsewhere in detail, as culminating in the dithyramb "The Fire Beacon."[18] While he was still in a hopeful, elated frame of mind, Nietzsche dwelled on the possibility of hauling in a catch from the human sea, which he also called the human abyss (*Menschen-Meer, Menschen-Abgrund*, op. cit). In the same spirit with which he called for a new justice with regard to individual moralities and a sustaining sun for every individual, to provide warmth in spite of one's distance from the herd, he renewed the cry in "The Honey Sacrifice." This time he made clear that *his*

own was also at stake in the activity of fishing: "And what in all seas belongs
to me, my in-and-of-myself in all things—fish *that* out for me, bring *that* up
to me. . . . O how many seas are around me, and how many dawning futures
of man!"[19] Once more we have the dawning of human futures in connection
with mankind coming into its own as a result of the experience of the sea.
Zarathustra's was not a mission of saving or redeeming mankind; his motives
were not altruistic. Instead, Zarathustra as the fisher of men is the personifica-
tion of danger who wishes to lure men to their own destinies, and his role is to
coax men away from the herd. Left to their own devices in the moral wilder-
ness, men will come into their own. Zarathustra is merely the one who will
tempt them to explore the human sea, what is open, the human abyss; at stake
is the discovery of the self, but, without risking the voyage and possible
shipwreck as well, there is nothing.

Nietzsche stuck with the symbolism of the sea and seafaring into the period
of *Beyond Good and Evil.* In a fragment from that period (summer 1985) used
in part as *Beyond* number 44 from "The Free Spirit," the historical Columbus
is placed into a futuristic context that spells out how Nietzsche charged the
symbol with meaning. The rather long discussion begins with a question that
had concerned Nietzsche since at least *On the Advantage and Disadvantage of
History for Life*—namely: how should the species man stand in relation to his
earth in an extranational and extraracial sense? The overman was the biggest
step in this direction of thinking, and we will recognize one of his characteris-
tics in the new breed of man discussed in the fragment; he opposes the herd
morality and proposes danger instead of security. Europe's "free spirits" had
not been free enough, but in their partial success they went as far as becoming
idealists, artists, and critics. These types never attempted the consequential
difference, however, which was "a reversal of values" (*Umkehrung der
Werte*). Closest in this regard would have been the critic-historian who began
"the discovery of the old world—it is the work of the *new* Columbus, of the
German spirit. . . . For indeed, in the old world a different, a more masterful
morality reigned than today; and the man of antiquity, under the educating
power of his morality, was a stronger and deeper man than the man of
today."[20] In a moment of rare praise for the critic-historian, who is personified
as a new Columbus representing the enterprising German spirit, Nietzsche
recognized that the portal to antiquity had been opened, and, most important
for his own purpose and hopes, the portal to a culture that was not paralyzed
by its moral teachings.[21] The German spirit in the tradition of Winckelmann
and his later orbit had been doing the work of Columbus, but as a new
discoverer who pointed out the "old world" cast off by post-Renaissance
Europe. By following in the spirit of the new Columbus, which entails a
return to pre-Christian values based on mastery (*Herrschaft*), one circumnavi-

gates the globe of history and eventually becomes free, that is, arrives at the source or comes into one's own. The symbolic journey by sea is the experience of living beyond the pale of Europe's old values, plus the creative work of positing one's self in the place made open by the falling away of intervening Christian history.

Clearly, there is a rich background to Nietzsche's tiny poem in "Songs of Prince Free as a Bird," entitled "To New Seas."[22] It is the only published version of the poem and by no means the best one. In all there are seven versions; five are found in the *Studienausgabe* of Colli and Montinari, one is included in "Free as a Bird," and the remaining version is found in the Naumann edition of 1906 (vol. 8). Among the different arrangements Nietzsche preferred this first stanza (cross rhyme in the original):

> *Freundin*—spoke Columbus—heed!
> Trust no more the Genoese!
> Off he stares into the azure,
> Lured too much by distant seas![23]

This version was entitled "On the High Sea" and consisted of only two strophes. The second reads:

> Whom he loves, he lures with pleasure
> Far beyond both space and time—
> Above us star by star is gleaming,
> 'Round us roars eternity. (ibid.)

What emerges in this version is the idea of luring; Columbus himself is lured by the sea, which makes him a dangerous companion who would prefer the distant to the close.

Columbus is also the one who lures others, for, in loving another, Columbus the discoverer of the new moral order would lure her/him beyond the reach of safety *for one's own sake,* "far beyond both space and time." In his role as Zarathustra-Columbus, the explorer shows his love not by sheltering others, as is the case among altruistic Christians, but by exposing others to the unknown; this is the symbolic journey necessary in Nietzsche's thinking that one makes in order to divest oneself of the collective (herd) mentality. The relatively complete version of the poem entitled "Yorick-Columbus" has four strophes, but the first is the same. Strophe two begins: "What is most foreign I treasure most! / Genoa—that sank, and disappeared— . . ." In addition to confessing his preference for what is most foreign, we learn that Genoa, the seaport home of Columbus, is gone and no longer is a factor. This is why the third strophe reads "Hither I want to go—now I trust / Myself henceforth, and my ship."[24] One does not necessarily have a destination, only the need to venture forth, and all one can rely on is the self. The element of novelty in keeping with the New World emerges in the final strophe:

> Everything grows newer to me,
> Far beyond gleam space and time—
> And the fairest monster laughing
> Beckons there: eternity.

Nietzsche was convinced that upon abandoning our herd morality an entire new world of possibilities would open up, possibilities that could well be called existential possibilities as expressions of uninhibited human self-determination. The sea monster one encounters on the Nietzschean passage is eternity, the greatest fear of the European, Christian man, as long as he remains within the herd; otherwise, and as a result of having ventured forth into danger and having found his own, the seafarer will recognize eternity in the spirit of affirmation connected with the eternal recurrence of the same—it is only a horror for those who cling to the past, who have not experienced the glorious moment of living that makes eternal recurrence an attractive, challenging proposition.

At various times the poem was entitled "To ————," "To New Seas," "Columbus Novus," "On the High Sea," "Out to Sea," "Yorick-Columbus" and "The New Columbus."[25] Any versions of the poem, even the longest of four strophes, will appear as innocent *Kreuzreim* to the reader who is unfamiliar with Nietzsche's method of symbolizing philosophy. In the Columbus poems Nietzsche brought together in abbreviated, lyrical form those associations that stress the importance of departure from the collective in order to come into one's own. The journey by sea, as opposed to any other journey, is regarded by the poet as a trial worthy of the human spirit, and capable of separating what is common to all, or none, from what is uniquely one's own. Furthermore, one's own, in Nietzschean and Heideggerian parlance, is not simply a matter of having chosen an interesting path, nor having chosen to appear different, nor having imposed isolation upon oneself for the sake of ascetic exercise; one's own is the breakthrough to selfhood, capable of being defined only by virtue of individual trial, and worthy enough to have as its source of illumination its own, self-sustaining sun. As in most Nietzschean writing, the Columbus idea is a contribution to the *Auseinandersetzung* with moral philosophy; this manner of philosophizing, in turn, is not restricted to any pursuit of absolutes but intends to suspend morality in favor of discovering or revealing the essentially human. It has been seen that Hölderlin had a profound concern for the essentially human; his manner of pursuing what is one's own, however, bears little resemblance to Nietzsche's oppositional strategies and does not have behind it the multifaceted campaign to transvaluate values under the banner of an active nihilism. Community remains in Hölderlin, but for Nietzsche it is equated with the herd.

When we follow the chronology of Hölderlin's correspondence, we learn that the theme of the sea and images of seafaring play a vital role in his perception of the poet. Perhaps the earliest expression of the association between the seafarer and the poet was in the early hymn to Columbus, which was written sometime in 1789, but which is now lost.[26] A few years later, again in a letter to his friend and fellow-poet Neuffer, Hölderlin responded enthusiastically to his friend's claim that much remained to be said in the medium of poetry, and surely a wealthy field of discovery lay before him. He continued: "What you say so beautifully about the *terra incognita* in the realm of poetry applies precisely to the novel in particular. There are predecessors enough, but few who succeeded in discovering new, beautiful land, and there is still an immensity for discovery and treatment!"[27] At this point in his letter Hölderlin promised his friend that the novel *Hyperion,* which was not yet completed, would be worthy of their sentiments or he would consign it to the flames. Especially revealing here is Hölderlin's symbol for the mission of the poet; terra incognita, with its potential to disclose new land, also contributes to the further animation of being through man's added dimension, the "treatment" of this new land as the material addressed by poets.

Hölderlin continued to associate the mission of exploration with the poet's vocation as seen in his letter of 20 January 1797 to his mother; for years Hölderlin had avoided accepting a pastorship and settling down into a domestic relationship. One could scarcely urge another to return to port, he argued, before the journey was half over.[28] There is more at stake here than just another argument, or plea, to remain unattached and unencumbered by the demands of a false career choice, though frequently in his letters to his mother we find Hölderlin engaging in this activity. The analogy of returning to port before the journey is completed tells us something about Hölderlin's conception of the poet's calling. He does not know exactly where the journey will take him, nor does he know whether the journey will culminate successfully; what he knows, however, is that the journey must be ventured and he must follow through.

Just a couple of weeks later he used similar language in a letter to Neuffer. "I have sailed around a world of joy since we last wrote. . . . The waves bore me away; my entire nature was always too much in life to reflect upon itself." This served as an explanation for why Hölderlin did not write sooner to tell about himself, and it reflects the joy of his early Frankfurt period and the love for Susette Gontard (Diotima), which he had to keep secret. In confessing that the waves simply bore him away, Hölderlin expressed his proximity to the sailor's mentality; while "at sea" during his joyful circumnavigation (the

Frankfurt period was his most productive), he was characteristically too wrapped up in living to reflect upon himself and send news to the friend. This involvement in life, however, was not always a pleasure cruise. Hölderlin closed his letter by remarking how the gods provide great joy *and* great sorrow for the ones they love, ostensibly the poets, and he well understood that setting sail on a brook is no great feat: "but when our heart and destiny hurl us down to the bottom of the sea, and up to the heavens, that makes the helmsman."[29] The experience of the high and dangerous seas, as opposed to dwelling at home, is the measure of the true poet as well as the true helmsman.

After the joy of the Frankfurt period began to wear thin, and Hölderlin's duties as tutor in the Gontard household became more and more difficult to face, he wrote cautionary remarks to his younger brother on 14 March 1798.[30] The poet's calling troubled him deeply now and would continue to do so; one must avoid trading prematurely one's "beautiful lively nature" for the struggle and ambition encountered beyond youth. In making this warning he was aware that he sounded like one who "had suffered shipwreck" and therefore cautioned others to stay in port until safe weather for sailing. For his part he had evidently ventured forth too early and would pay for it his whole life long.[31] Surely this letter expressed one of the abysmal lows of Hölderlin's journey as poet-helmsman.

As we follow the course of the navigation symbol through Hölderlin's correspondence, keeping in mind that he was unable to divulge his private relationship to friends and family—because his beloved "Diotima" was in reality Susette Gontard, the wife of his employer—we glimpse the personal dimension of associations that emerge so successfully in the poetry. Even in Nietzsche's strict terms, Hölderlin was one who embarked on the discovery of new lands. And though certainly Nietzsche did not wish to give Hölderlin credit, it was Hölderlin who discovered the new "old world" of antiquity and made it his mission to test himself against the unknown, against sea and sky. Heedless of the danger to himself, and by his own standards having become shipwrecked as a consequence of launching his voyage prematurely—without the proper auspices—Hölderlin clearly exemplified the heroic ideal that Nietzsche claimed for himself.

Hölderlin began to use the image of the sailor returning to port as early as "Evening Phantasy" (ca. 1799), and he continued to elaborate this theme into the period of the very last fragments of hymns, as seen in "Columbus."[32] The peacefulness, togetherness enjoyed by all at the close of day is accentuated by the first lines of the strophe: "Surely now the sailors return to port, / In distant cities. . . ."[33] Hölderlin had begun the poem with a very close image, the plowman in the shadow of his cottage, his stove alight. The strophe's closing lines expand the image to the wanderer's reception in a peaceful village; a welcoming evening bell tolls him into the community. The image is finally expanded beyond the presently familiar with the use of "surely now the sailors return," expressing probability as perceived by the poet, who everywhere sees and imagines humble, industrious people returning from their day labors. This element of having earned a respite after an honest day's work is completely absent in Nietzsche, since he attributes little or no value to the communal pursuits of man.

A similar treatment of the sailor occurs, as we have seen, in the ode "The Homeland," where the poet wrote:

> Cheerfully the sailor turns home on the still river,
> From islands far away, when he has harvested;
> So would I too come home, had I
> Harvested goods so many as sorrows.[34]

Once again the vocation of the sailor is juxtaposed with the poet's; the sailor "harvests" and returns with his goods which could be his catch of fish, his discoveries, his experiences. A subtlety is introduced here as well; Hölderlin wishes he could return as cheerfully as the sailor, he wishes that his numerous sorrows were instead his goods. There is a conscious association of the harvest of sorrow with the harvest of the sailors, so that the poet must now begin to view his vocation as similar to the sailor's but resulting, for now, in a different catch, in different goods. What Hölderlin senses as lacking up to this point is his own, his place, his "proper measure" in life. He is capable of reflecting with some longing on the vocation of the sailor because he senses a kinship with him; the sailor must leave the safety of his home and the land behind, but, upon returning, he is not empty handed. Hölderlin saw the poet at various times as one who brings near what is furthest, as in the example of the poet's role as mediator between men and gods. The journey of the poet into the unknown is undertaken in order to discover himself, which will enable him to bear the vocation of the poet with the same propriety enjoyed by homecoming sailors. The sailors return cheerfully not only because they have brought home a rich harvest but because they _are coming home_ and have missed their home in the interval of the journey. Or as Heidegger has written in connection with "Remembrance," Hölderlin's greatest completed hymn featuring the theme of sea travel, "the sojourn in foreign places and the alienation [_Befremdung_] in foreign places have to be, so that what is proper [_das Eigene_] about the foreign places begins to show [_leuchten_]. . . . The sea journey thus stands beneath the concealed law of the homecoming into what is proper."[35]

Heidegger's seemingly cryptic remarks, with their suggestive rather than concrete terminology, demonstrate both the Nietzschean and Hölderlinian influence. While Heidegger accepts the usefulness of Nietzsche's oppositional strategy, summarized in the need to leave the collective in order to get at one's own through the experience of the unknown, he seems to prefer Hölderlin's definition of the point of departure and the point of return. *Das Eigene* is therefore inherent in the strange places, as is the case with Nietzsche, but, unlike Nietzsche, *das Eigene* retains no value unless it makes its way home. This "home" in the case of Hölderlin, in turn, cannot be a real home without the proper influx or measure of the foreign element that shapes the poet and makes him a spokesman for his community.

Hölderlin stated the relationship between seafarers and the gods in "The Archipelago." A long strophe is introduced with the question, "Say, where is Athens?" Has it sunk into ashes, he asks, "Or is there still a sign of her, that perhaps the sailor, / When he passes by, may name and think of her?"[36] The sailor has a special relationship with Athens and the islands of Greece; both Aeneas and Jason are lauded in "Columbus," and, in historic terms, ancient Greece is the port from which Greek culture and the gods spread across the sea and Europe. In Hölderlin's thinking, as well as in the minds of several contemporaries and successors, Greece was the source; those who remain cognizant of her, and are able to recognize and name her, are sailors, or, in Hölderlin's case, poets who keep the memory alive by virtue of their vocation. The poet continues

> Behold! the distant-thinking merchant launched his ship,
> Glad, for the winged airs blow also for him and the gods
> Loved him, as the poet, as well, while he balanced
> The good gifts of the earth and united distant with near. (Ibid.)

In these lines we see underscored the analogy of the poet with the sailor and merchant; the merchant, too, thinks in terms of distance and is happy for favorable winds. The gods, furthermore, love him as they love the poet, for the merchant strikes a balance among things, prices and prizes them, making them available and thereby uniting the distant with the near. What is proper to the merchant is the venturing forth in order to gather the earth's goods, the balancing or weighing of their merits, and the overall process of bringing home or exporting from home what is to be shared. In "The Archipelago" Hölderlin has completed the identification of the poet and the seafarer; as gatherers, they are close to the gods, and, as gatherers, they more than any others make intelligible what is proper to men and gods.

"Remembrance" begins:

> The north-east wind blows,
> Dearest of the winds

To me, because he promises fiery spirit
And good voyage to the sailors.[37]

The northeast wind is beloved by the sailors for its favorable direction, be-
loved by the poet because it comes to the aid of sailors—which is to say, it
comes to his aid as well when we follow Hölderlin's established association
between sailor and poet. The real and symbolic sea of the poet's thoughts lies
after all to the south. The fourth strophe of the hymn merits quoting in its
entirety:

> But where are the friends? Bellarmin
> With the companion? Many a man
> Shies away from going to the source;
> Wealth namely begins
> In the sea. They
> Like painters, bring together
> The beauty of the earth and disdain
> Not the winged war, and
> Living alone, years at a time, beneath
> The leafless mast, where the night is not brightened
> By the holidays of the city,
> And the music of strings and the dance of natives. (Ibid.)

In so offering several details of the sailor's isolation and how he must per-
severe without the comforts afforded those who remain at home, we are
reminded of Nietzsche's seafaring quest for the new moral world; specifically,
we recall that Nietzsche had praised the German spirit for discovering the old
world in its role as the new Columbus—this old world is the world of the
ancients, whose "masterful culture" Nietzsche considered superior to modern
European culture. "Many a man / Shies away from going to the source,"
wrote Hölderlin in connection with seafaring and *the beginning of wealth in
the sea.* In Nietzsche's case, the source is Greece (in historical terms) and, if
Hölderlin does not specifically isolate Greece as the source in "Re-
membrance," we still have to consider the sea as the symbol of the poet's
journey in a manner consistent with Nietzsche's thinking. The lines "Wealth
namely begins / In the sea," which is why the sailors, merchants, and poets
embark in the first place, also remind us of Nietzsche-Zarathustra's words that
the world is "an abysmal wealthy sea" from which he hopes to haul in the
catch, which is his own proper self, "my in-and-of-myself in all things."[38]
Hölderlin's seafarers make the great sacrifice of distance, solitude, dark-
ness, and barrenness, but they are gatherers who bring in the goods and
beauties of the earth. Unlike Nietzsche's existential sailor, what is brought
back is to be shared; it has collective value as goods, just as merchants

bridge distances in order to introduce goods among the people, where the value "good" takes shape and preserves its meaning. What's more, while Hölderlin's seafarer is away from the collective, celebration with its music and dancing goes on. At least two important distinctions are evident here. First, the work or harvest of the sailor contributes to the celebration of those who remain at home, for they are to be enriched by the treasures brought back. And second, Hölderlin's sailors do not go forth as exiles, voluntary or otherwise; they go forth because it is their calling, because their propriety (*Eigenes*) demands this of them, and because they, too, believe in celebration and wish to be favored by gods. In other words, by coming into their own, the sailors of Hölderlin's mind also help others to come into their own; there is a close tie between serving the community and serving the gods who confer legitimacy to Hölderlin's profound notion of community. One gets the impression that the sacrifice of Hölderlin's voyager is more immediate, and more real, than the sacrifice of Nietzsche's, because for Hölderlin there is already an authentic existence at work among the people, who are not berated as herd animals. This existence depends inextricably on the courage and success of the voyager, so that he literally misses what is going on at home, but, even in his absence, or let us say, *precisely* in his absence, he enriches the community.

In the final strophe of "Remembrance," we learn that the men have gone to the Indians, where Columbus was supposed to have landed. The concluding sentence reads:

> but the sea
> Takes and gives memory,
> And love also fixes the gaze intently,
> What endures, though, the poets ordain.

The sea takes memory in the sense that it temporarily possesses or occupies the sailors; while at sea, man must reckon only with the sea, battle the winds, harness them, suspend any rules that apply while men are on land. It is not the individual memory of the sailor per se that is at stake here but the memory that preserves the gods in the spirit of gathering and uniting near and far, which is proper to the sailor. The celebrations that the sailor forgoes are only possible because they are gifts of the gods, with their music, wine, and dancing offered votively to the gods whose presence is established among mortals because the poet/sailor has ventured forth into the open. This moving on, as it was called in "Bread and Wine," is a mortal activity, but one touched, animated, by the gods who coexist with man.

That love plays a role here is not surprising, because the unwavering gaze of love, or the lover, is what strikes a link all around; the gods gaze upon man, man gazes upon the sea from the land and hopes for the return of the loved one, and sailors gaze upon the sea and the lands (for example, Greece, and in order to sight land); and in this unwavering gaze of love the memory of what was and what must continue to be is sustained by common effort. When the poet concludes, "What endures, though, the poets ordain," he is once again citing the brotherhood of voyager and poet; the sailor has gathered, returned with the earth's good, but the poet is the one who must establish what remains—that is, it depends on him to work with the harvest in such a way that the people are kept awake, and the presence of the gods is preserved.

The relationship cited in the foregoing discussion also occurs in "Columbus," in such a way as to shed light on the activity we have described as establishing what is proper. Sieburth uses the _Frankfurter Ausgabe_ version of the poem, as Beissner's is all too truncated, but we must keep in mind that even the version preferred by Sieburth is fragmentary.[39] The poet begins by stating that, if he had his choice of what manner of hero he could be, "then it would be a sea hero." But it is not adventure that the poet is looking for; Heidegger had already ruled out this aspect in his sensitive treatment of "Remembrance."[40] Instead, the poet clarifies that "homely dwelling and order" are essential to decipher the arid beauty and the figures burnt into sand, as well as a good telescope and education, "namely for life / To inquire of the heavens." The seafaring explorer is in an environment much like the desert, where only sharp eyes perceive nuances, but observe also that he is a valuable man of the land, pointing out Hölderlin's belief that the poet must be intelligible to his community, responsible to it, as the matter of questioning the heavens is not undertaken for personal gain or edification.

Later on in the poem, the narrator's voice becomes Columbus's; he is critical of the trepidation and posturing of those who are among his men preparing for voyage.[41]

> I am troubled by this little
> Patience and benevolence my judge and protector god
> For we are men
> And they would believe they were monks.
> And one, as spokesman
> Stepped before us as preacher
> In his blue jerkin
> . . . .
>
> But out yonder, so that
> From here
> We can move, therefore cried
> Mightily judging
> The companions the voice of the sea god,
> The pure voice, by which
> Heroes recognize whether they justly
> Succeed or not[42]

Columbus is critical of the lack of patience and goodwill that influences his crew. The clergyman orator, in particular, decked out in blue but, apparently, no match for the limitless blue of the sea, underscores the irrelevance of pious words at this moment. The crew will be called upon, literally, to demonstrate under stress what is of man, not what is proper to monks in their protected environment. In his thoughts Columbus calls upon his "judge and protector god," which in this case represents his own, heroic perception of God and God's work, or, perhaps even, the sea god. In any case, the voice that calls louder than all others is the voice of the sea, "mightily judging" and "pure" as befitting a sea god. In this matter, which is the preparation for venturing forth into the unknown against all odds and the counsel of timid men, the gods can be heard only by those whose calling brings them nearer to the dwelling of the gods, or by those who are beloved of the gods and risk their own in order to contribute to the greater glory of men and gods. We are reminded of Hölderlin's words in "The Sanctimonious Poets," for here is a situation in which pious words are contrasted with the deeds of men of faith.

Columbus's faith is in learning and in daring men. During the voyage his sailors may have doubted, but not he: "Columbus however to himself hypostatization of the previous orbis / Naiveté of science."[43] What he criticizes in his aside is the hypostatization of the Old World's conception of the earth, which would cast in stone the superstitions of old and frame them in the name of science. A bit later,

Now they saw

There were namely many,
Of the beautiful islands.

therewith

With Lisbon

And Genoa shared;

For alone one
Can not bear the wealth from
The heavenly; indeed however may

A demigod stretch
        the harness, for the Highest though
Is almost too little
The working   where the daylight shines,
And the moon.[44]

Some work is in order to provide a context for these fragmentary thoughts. The wealth in the form of numerous beautiful islands is a gift of the gods and, therefore, too big for any mortal to bear alone; this thought follows the sharing of the discovery by Lisbon and Genoa. When we speak of bearing (*tragen*), it is consistent to use the image of the harness, which stretches across the back or spans the shoulders. This harness could indeed be stretched or borne by a demigod, and Hölderlin may have referred to Columbus as a demigod in the manner of his friend Heinse.[45] As god and man, the demigod is precisely the one to fulfill the mission of bringing what is distant and what is near together in one place, delighting gods and men.

By naming Lisbon, Columbus's port of departure, and Genoa, his home, the poet establishes a link between two great seaports and also between the seafarer and his roots on the land. In the undertaking of the expedition, Genoa and Lisbon have joined forces, signifying that truly great actions in the community of men cannot take place in isolation. In the act of discovery, the void of suspended communication between gods (the wealth of the sea) and men is gloriously filled, each comes into his own in the moment of approaching. In the case of man, a new world is opened up, his isolation is diminished, contact is established with distant brethren, and the entire planet has become open. The gods, too, have come into their own, for their isolation is likewise diminished; communication between men and gods is brought about by the enterprising spirits—the seafarers, merchants, and poets—and the implication is that this spirit will now dwell in the New Worlds. One New World is the newly discovered half, the other is the newly constituted whole, completing for the first time in history the physical and spiritual journey of man in search of man.

Epilogue: On Freedom, Servitude, and Poetry

"The Work of the Poet" is the title of the first half of this study because Hölderlin did more than merely prescribe, in theoretical writing, what the poet is supposed to do; it is in the poetry itself, executed as the poet's work, that we find a unity illustrative of the unique and difficult vocation. Hölderlin wrote theoretical prose, and, in particular, an essay on the poetic process, but his writing here is turgid and confused. The opening sentence is by itself nearly two pages long, consisting of labyrinthine conditionals, and the instruction one gleans from this exercise in patience is minute in comparison to the manifest value inherent in the poems themselves. I agree with Harold Bloom that what a *poet* has to say about poetry is said in his poetry: "The poet's conception of himself is his poem's conception of itself. . . ."[1] Hölderlin speaks more eloquently, and with greater harmony, in his poetry than one would ever expect from having followed the meandering course of his life, with its many ups and downs, with its constant self-doubt. As Adolf Beck points out in his commentary to the correspondence, what the poet had to repress concerning his private life, including the single great love for his Diotima, was expressed all the more forcefully in the poetry, where the other Hölderlin is at work.[2] Apparently, Nietzsche was not the only poet "at two" with himself, even while he longed to be at one, as he lamented in the illuminating dithyramb "Mere Fool! Mere Poet!"

Hölderlin's letters reveal how from the earliest days he wrestled with the alternating patterns of freedom and servitude, and it is not at all surprising to find a willingness to engage and resolve these tensions in the poems. The question of freedom in Hölderlin's life does not formulate itself as a strident anti, nor does it assume the dimensions of an escape. Here Nietzsche becomes helpful, for he, too, struggled with gaining freedom without compromise; his prophet Zarathustra got right to the matter:

> Free you call yourself? I want to hear your ruling
> thought, and not that you escaped from a yoke.
> Are you one who had a *right* to escape the yoke?
> There are many who threw away their last value when
> they threw away their servitude.[3]

Servitude was hateful to Hölderlin, and he surely believed he had the right to escape from the yoke, indeed, a far greater right and duty to remove the yoke from all burdened men.

Charles Taylor introduces his *Hegel* with an essay on expression and freedom as the dominating thoughts at the close of the eighteenth century in Germany. In terms that apply particularly well to Hölderlin, he writes that for "intellectual Germans of the 1790s these two ideas, expression and radical freedom, took on a tremendous force. It was born partly no doubt of the changes in German society which made the need for a new identity to be felt all the more pressingly." And though both Karl Marx and Heinrich Heine had said it in their day, Taylor correctly stresses that the character and situation of the Germans, combined with the political disappointment of the French Revolution, made it almost inevitable that the Revolution would be carried into the sphere of culture, from politics to philosophy, in Germany.[4] The Kantian radical freedom, which encourages individual autonomy, and Herder's expressive freedom, which encourages the unity of man with nature in and through art, were factors very much on the mind of Hölderlin. It was imperative for him to remain free, to be receptive only to what he considered divine nature's promptings, while at the same time, in attempting to enact freedom in his art, as expression, he was hampered by those day-to-day factors that eroded his gains. Within himself there were obstacles to overcome, incongruities to reconcile, so that he could hardly represent himself as a unified front. From without, there were again factors that worked negatively upon him, aggravating the tension within himself. In a sense, the turmoil of Hölderlin's inner life, which served as the grist for his reconciling poetry, made him keenly aware of compromise, of servitude, and it seemed these were always too close for comfort.

Let us first consider the inner conflict as it contributed to the freedom/servitude complex. In one of his first remarks on choosing a profession, he wrote to his mother that teaching would one day become his main occupation.[5] As matters turned out, teaching as a private tutor was Hölderlin's occupation, though by no means a regular one, and he never regarded it as a vocation so much as it afforded him the liberty of *not* accepting a pastorship or other clerical assignment. For example, five years later, again in a letter to his mother, Hölderlin explained that he would rather find a tutorial position (*Hofmeister*), which would enable him to be on his own, than to move back to Nürtingen, where he would live with his mother; he reasoned that people would only accuse him of being a good-for-nothing who consumed his mother's food, and, if he did not locate a private position soon, the consistory would demand that he accept their assignment. This must have been a very real threat to Hölderlin, who after all had graduated from the famous Tübinger Stift in theology and was supposed to have become a pastor.[6]

It was through Schiller's direct intervention that Hölderlin had received his first tutorial position, and one could say that it was Hölderlin's preference to follow in the footsteps of the poet Schiller that made tutoring a mere convenience and not a vocation. Two professions, therefore, seemed to lay claim to his future energies; tutoring kept him beyond the reach of the consistory, without providing the atmosphere he required to be at peace with himself, while each time he gave up a tutorship he felt forced to scramble for another one just to assert his independence from the profession for which he had trained. Both the consistory and Hölderlin's mother exerted pressure in this area, and the balancing act was always costly.

Remaining free in this dubious manner came at the expense of the real vocation, the poet's, and that could scarcely flourish with the internal strife that characterized Hölderlin's personality from the outset. To Louise Nast he confessed in March 1790 that the major cause of his ceaseless melancholy was frustrated ambition; a year later he divulged to his sister that what he really wanted to do was live in peace and privacy, writing books and, he hoped, not starving.[7] Just a few months later he explained to his mother that his restless character, moodiness, plans, and ambition would never allow him to settle into a quiet, married life and a pastorship; already the poet knew himself quite well, and his remarks were prophetic.[8] From now on there would be growing turmoil over the inability to devote himself full time to writing.

As a consequence of not having enough time, nor the proper atmosphere in which to develop as a poet, Hölderlin began to have doubts about his vocation even as his wishes were partially, and modestly, fulfilled. In January of 1795 he was able to tell Neuffer that his publisher (arranged again by Schiller) was awarding him an honorarium for the first volume of *Hyperion,* so that he could look forward to living in peace and independence for the summer.[9] Indeed, when Hölderlin was not receiving money from the publishers, or when his salary as a tutor did not suffice, he had to turn to his mother for financial support—not a happy arrangement for one so sensitive to the issue of maintaining his autonomy. Early in 1797 he wrote from Frankfurt that his poetry now "has more life and form; my imagination is more willing to adopt the forms of the world, my heart is full of enthusiasm." But already by July of the same year, possibly as a reflection of growing tensions in the Gontard household, he expressed envy to Neuffer that the friend's existence was based on other activities besides writing, while he, Hölderlin, ruined everything that he might otherwise do and only infrequently enjoyed the success of a few good lines of poetry.[10]

In spite of the obstacles to freeing himself for his vocation, Hölderlin showed signs of hardening resolve during the late Frankfurt period, which was perhaps the saddest time of his life since it held only the prospect of another abandoned tutorship and a wrecked love life. In connection with the forthcoming second volume of *Hyperion,* he related to his brother that he was "rather in opposition to the current ruling taste, but even in future I will not abandon my stubbornness, and hope to fight my way through."[11] We have seen that, by opposition to the ruling taste, Hölderlin meant that his writing would not be a commentary on other poets and their works but an exploration of the terra incognita he and his friends believed lay beyond the mainland.

There were times when Hölderlin blamed his poetic dissatisfaction on the generally unhealthy climate for poetry, and on his own compensating fluctuation. This very revealing observation was made to his brother on 12 February 1798:

> Do you know the root of all my evils? I wish to live the art on which I have set my heart, and must work my way around, among people, so that I am often quite weary of life. And why? Because art provides for the master, but not for the disciple. But this I say only to you. I am a weak hero, am I not, that I do not go out and conquer the freedom that I need. But see, dear brother, then I would be living at war again, and that is not favorable to art, either. Let it be then! Many a man has already perished who was made to be a poet. We do not live in the poet's climate. For this reason scarcely one of ten such plants survives.[12]

The lyrical expression of this sentiment emerges in "Bread and Wine" with the famous words "and wherefore poets in paltry times?" But unlike the letter to his brother, which suggests inadequacy as a poet, "Bread and Wine" survives as an unparalleled expression of art providing for the master.

When Hölderlin fled to Homburg in 1798 his private life was in tatters and his sense of poetic vocation seriously wounded. He wrote to Neuffer that he was a failed poet and one who could always flee to philosophy as though to a hospital. In this dark, depressed frame of mind he claimed he would rather perish anonymously than leave "the sweet home of the muses, from which mere chance has banished me." In an outpouring of his poetic ambivalence, this time to his mother just two months later, he detailed at length how his ill humor and dissatisfaction derived from working too closely with philosophy whenever he tried to compensate for lack of poetic success; philosophy was not his element, and it only aggravated his moods. From here he went on to discuss the possibility of accepting a pastorship, for he had learned that the professions do not tolerate mixing.[13] We can infer that his dissatisfaction with poetry was indeed great at this time, since it was expressed in these terms to his mother.

But there is more at stake than Hölderlin's lack of fulfillment and his perceptions of failure, whether measured in his terms or society's (which he did not clearly separate). The striving to synthesize expressive freedom and moral freedom, as outlined so skillfully by Taylor, is also in evidence here. Hölderlin was willing to recognize no master but nature, and when nature did not speak clearly through him, as the medium of expressive freedom, then he felt put upon by outside factors and attempted to extricate himself through philosophical reflection. But reflection as the vehicle for moral freedom must be accompanied by the unified, natural self as expression, in order to effect what Taylor calls "a higher synthesis in which both harmonious unity and full self-consciousness would be united." The poets of the 1790s wished neither to lose themselves in nature, thereby sacrificing reflection and moral freedom, nor to lose themselves in reflection, thereby sacrificing expressive freedom.[14] We know that Hölderlin was intimately aware of this problem as a theoretical and a personal manifestation, for he had studied the philosophy of Kant, Fichte, and Schiller, and was himself a contributing factor in the early writings of Schelling and Hegel.

A remark to Neuffer on 4 December 1799 sheds light on Hölderlin's mature perception of his place among the poets of the day. He began by doubting his own status as a poet, observing that it was virtually impossible to make a living as a poet without becoming all too subservient (*dienstbar*) and acting at the expense of one's reputation. Perhaps in his case a vicariate or *Hofmeister* position, or some lesser job in which he could devote time to writing, was the proper solution after all.[15] On the surface he seemed to be capitulating in the same spirit of resignation with which he had approached his mother, but by now we have seen too much of Hölderlin's struggle for autonomy to discount the remarks. The subservience he criticized, which might lead to success judged by another's standards but which would only compromise himself, is a dimension of servitude. The poet's code of honor, not merely two centuries ago but also today, could well be formulated as: make it yourself, or don't make it at all. Hölderlin knew that he was dangerously close in the waning years of the eighteenth century to compromising himself. He understood with poignancy that his reliance on the good graces of Schiller was not exactly in the manner of heroic defiance, and he was able to admit it to Schiller in several letters. When his efforts to obtain a position as lecturer at the university of Jena, through Schiller's intervention, were not successful, and, similarly, when Schiller counseled him not to establish a literary journal in which Hölderlin had placed great promise, he knew how much he would have had to depend on Schiller in each case. Freedom to pursue the poet's vocation should not be won by associating oneself too closely with another, and for Hölderlin, who obviously admired Schiller's ability to rise above the obstacles of sickness, lack of financial support, and the larger-than-life presence of Goethe, gaining that precious freedom was not so vital as keeping faith with himself.

If Hölderlin had reason to feel isolated among the poets of his day, notwithstanding Schiller's concrete and moral support, then at least he did not feel isolated in his proper task when he was carrying it out—that is, while he was writing poetry. In the poems he is situated between nature and man, between the gods and man, not in the sense that he is stranded there, in the interval, but as the operative factor in closing the interval and joining. Hölderlin is "open" in his poetry, as the true mediator should be open who exhorts his listeners to come and behold the open. There is a Kantian dimension to this quality, which emerges in a letter to his brother from 2 November 1797. He is recommending Kant and explains that, when he first began to read the philosopher, Kant had been as strange to him as any other person: "But each evening I had overcome new difficulties; that gave me an awareness of my freedom, and the consciousness of our freedom, our activity, in which it also expresses itself, is quite deeply related to the feeling of the higher, divine freedom, which is simultaneously the feeling of the most high, the most perfect."[16] It is this freedom that could not be compromised, and in the poetry we are often struck by the linkage of the poet's activity with the expression of the divine. Hölderlin's day-to-day world could only express this insight as a flash of communication, in prose, perhaps even in the recurring lament of not being sufficiently free while intuiting the freedom of which he knew.

The events of the poet's day-to-day, considered in the span of years that mark the beginning of his efforts to pursue his calling all the way to his mental collapse around 1806, present a picture out of focus. Hölderlin enjoyed artistic successes but never enough to settle him, and never enough to chase away the demons. There were many starts and false starts; there was sufficient range between the joys and sorrows to let the poet know he was favored by his gods, and all of this Hölderlin accepted as the poet's vocation. Holding to his notion of freedom, as Schiller had clearly embraced it also in his Kant-inspired philosophical essays, the poet brought his own fractured life into focus by translating, or transmitting, his association with the divine, with nature, into language. This transmittal, according to Ryan, is the role of the poet as seen in "As on a Holiday," where the communal spirit's thoughts culminate in the soul of the poet. Poetry holds the living energy of the storms, which churn up the lives of people, and in poetry, for the first time, these storms achieve an enduring and complete form that is otherwise denied them.[17]

We have followed this sign of the communal spirit through numerous Hölderlin texts and know that, just as it applies to the age in which the poet lived, it applied also to his own life and work, for Hölderlin was able to bear the vocation of the poet with greater dignity in his poetic expression, where it truly counts, than in his own brief and stormy existence. As an individual, he frequently reproached himself, despaired, and sought advice but was reluctant to give it when called upon. It was as if he knew the limitations of the individual while dealing in a medium that does not easily tolerate the individual. These remarks from 10 January 1798 to his brother-in-law, who had made Hölderlin one of the sponsors (godparents) of his second child, reinforce the understanding of freedom in relation to the communal spirit as the poet's primary responsibility: "I feel ever more how inseparably our work and life are associated with those powers which move about us, and so it is natural that I in no way consider it sufficient to create only out of oneself, and to throw one's individuality out blindly into the world, even if it were the most universally valid."[18]

As these words were offered in the religious context of becoming a sponsor for his nephew and Hölderlin's feeling a renewed love for life because of his attachment to this new life, we might dismiss the poet's words as perhaps being tailored for pious familial consumption. But Hölderlin's words would stand without the familial context as a faithful expression of his conception of the communal spirit. The genuine poet is not subjective; he does not write for the sake of describing himself or another, and no individuality (*Eigentümlichkeit*) is sufficiently interesting or universal to warrant its intrusion into the world. The faith in poetry, insofar as it is also a faith in the communal spirit, in the shared existence of gods and men, could actually grow in Hölderlin while his ties to the day-to-day world diminished. One could speak of a transfer of religious emotion here and not be totally wrong, but, as Taylor cautions with regard to the reception of Kant's radical freedom and its liberating but challenging effect on the generation of the 1790s, any authority "even as high as God himself, is condemned as heteronomy."[19] The freedom that Hölderlin celebrated in the poems is tantamount to the experience of self-overcoming.

It is on this note, the concept of self-overcoming, that a concluding word on freedom and poetry might benefit from a brief visit to the austere region of self-overcoming in the philosophy of Nietzsche. In his estimation, Hölderlin did not achieve that measure of self-overcoming that enables one to become sovereign. If we consider only the life of Hölderlin and judge him as he all too prematurely judged himself on this score, it would appear that he was not one of those few plants who survive the hostile climate for poetry. Such a judgment attaching only or primarily to the life of the poet is not proper, however, as our sojourn in the correspondence has shown. Nietzsche's focus was on the life, the records of events, activities, which is why he so admired Goethe; as the antiromantic who placed himself in the role of one who defrocks the poet/fool, Nietzsche remained reluctant to accept poetry as the measure of self-overcoming. This view was of course moderated when it came time to singing his own praises as a writer (especially with regard to his *Zarathustra*), but, generally speaking, he attributed his own self-overcoming to having successfully administered a rigorous "self-treatment" in order to overcome his own "illness" of romanticism. It is as though Nietzsche had to recreate himself according to his own image, so that the locus of self-overcoming remains in a new self, and self-overcoming moves from self to self.

Hölderlin's self-overcoming does not culminate in a new self, nor was his stress in life to "cure" himself, purge himself of pathological qualities. As a believer in poetry, and as one who was able to recognize the greatness of man through poetry—that activity that properly defines man—the self-overcoming means just that: the self, which from the outset is at odds with the other and itself, is overcome when the turmoil of existence is hypostatized as poetry. In the poems what had been fragmented and torn becomes whole; in the poems what had been the laboring struggle to get free becomes freedom.

Notes

Introduction

1. Harold Bloom, *Deconstruction and Criticism* (New York: Seabury Press, 1979), 17–18.

2. See Richard Unger's excellent introduction to *Friedrich Hölderlin* (Boston: Twayne Publishers, 1984), 1–14.

3. Charles Taylor, *Hegel and Modern Society* (Cambridge U.P., 1979), 2.

4. Paul de Man, *Blindness and Insight* (New York: Oxford U.P., 1971), 167.

5. Alice A. Kuzniar, *Delayed Endings: Nonclosure in Novalis and Hölderlin* (Athens: U. of Georgia P., 1987), 166.

6. de Man, 167.

7. M. B. Benn, *Hölderlin and Pindar* (The Hague: Mouton, 1962), 75.

8. This early reception I have outlined in "Reception and Impact: The First Decade of Nietzsche in Germany," *Orbis Litterarum* (1982), vol. 37, 32–46.

9. One should turn to the fourth part of *Zarathustra,* to the so-called magician's song, which was included among the *Dionysus Dithyrambs* as "Mere Fool! Mere Poet."

10. Erich Heller and Anthony Thorlby, "Idealism and Religious Vision in the Poetry of Hölderlin," *Quarterly Review of Literature* 10: 1 and 2 (1959), 33.

11. Friedrich Schiller, *Über die aesthetische Erziehung des Menschen in einer Reihe von Briefen* in *Schillers Werke in zwei Bänden,* ed. Erwin Ackerknecht (München: Droemersche Verlagsanstalt, 1954), vol. 2, 574, no. 6 of the "Aesthetic Letters." See my essay "Ethical Aesthetic: Schiller and Nietzsche as Critics of the Eighteenth Century," *Germanic Review* 55: 2 (1980), 55–63.

12. Friedrich Nietzsche, *Die Geburt der Tragödie* in *Werke in drei Bänden,* ed. Karl Schlechta (München: Hanser, 1966), vol. 1, 61, section 10.

Chapter 1

1. Friedrich Hölderlin, "Die Eichbäume" in *Hölderlin, Sämtliche Werke, Bd. I. Gedichte bis 1800,* ed. Friedrich Beissner (Stuttgart: J. G. Cottasche Buchhandlung, 1946), vol. 1, pt. 1,

201. [Henceforth as vol., part (when the vol. has more than one part), and page—all preceded by GSA.]

2. GSA 1, 1, 255.

3. This is suggested by Günther Mieth, ed. *Friedrich Hölderlin Werke in zwei Bänden* (Stuttgart: Parkland, 1970), vol. 1, 457.

4. GSA 1, 1, 201.

5. Michael Hamburger discusses how Hölderlin relied on the power of love to alleviate spiritual servitude. See his *Hölderlin*, 2d ed. (London: The Harvill Press, 1952), 13.

6. Roughly paraphrased from W. K. C. Guthrie, *A History of Greek Philosophy* (Cambridge: Cambridge U. P., 1965), vol. 2, 141, 155, 123, 131.

7. GSA 1, 1, 240.

8. Ibid, 250.

9. Ibid.

10. This idea is given more personal expression in "Gods Once Wandered . . ." (*Götter wandelten einst . . .*) Speaking to his beloved "Diotima," the poet envisions a future world in which the gods have returned; they recognize that the lovers have created a secret world for themselves, out of love, known only to the gods, while those who concerned themselves only with mortal things are given to the earth. The divine regions of light are reserved for those who, through loving, preserve the relation between men and gods (274).

11. Ibid., 307. Michael Hamburger translates the title of this poem as "My Possessions," which I think is wrong for the following reasons. *Eigentum* means property in the sense that what is *eigen* to something is its proper-ness, as in the Latin *proprius*. In this case, the Latin root of property and the Germanic *eigen* correspond, so that "my possessions" materializes in an obvious way.

12. In support of my rendering *Eigentum* in this poem as property, consider Hölderlin's letter to Schiller on 4 September 1795: "I believe that this is the property [*Eigentum*] of rare persons, that they are able to give without receiving. . . ." (GSA 6, 1, 181).

13. Kuzniar, *Delayed Endings*, 161.

14. GSA 2, 1, 19. "*Gedichte nach 1800.*"

15. Ibid., 46.

16. Ibid., 48.

17. M. B. Benn, *Hölderlin and Pindar*, 107.

18. Benn and other commentators have pointed out that Hölderlin progressed deeper into the nature of poetry than his early mentor Schiller (see Benn, 107), but on this score it should be said in Schiller's behalf that the problem of mediating between gods and men was expressed by Schiller, however pedantically, in the poem "The Dividing of the Earth" (*Die Teilung der Erde*, 1795). Here Zeus has given the earth to various vocations, but the poet only shows up when it is too late, and all the vocations have been parceled out. The poet's explanation: he was occupied with Zeus, spending his time with the divine, which is the poet's natural preference. As a consolation, Zeus allows the poet "visiting rights" as frequently as he wishes, thereby establishing a place in the world for poetry, but one that is divorced from the normal affairs of men. Hölderlin could not settle for such a compromise, however, and this might serve as an example of the difference in temperament between the idealistic aesthetic of a Schiller and the ontological probing conducted by Hölderlin.

Chapter 2

1. GSA 1, 1, 241.

2. Ibid., 255.

3. Ibid., 257.

4. Friedrich Schlegel, *Kritische Fragmente* in *Kritische-Friedrich-Schlegel-Ausgabe,* ed. Hans Eichner and Ernst Behler (München: Schöningh, 1967), vol. 2, 182. The aphorism is no. 116 of *Das Athenäum.*

5. GSA 1, 1, 312.

Chapter 3

1. GSA 2, 1, 46.

2. At this point it is important to note that Hölderlin's favorite gods were actually demigods, that is, figures coexisting in the mortal and divine by virtue of their shared genesis. Hence, we find Hölderlin speaking in one breath about Dionysos and Christ, as figures with a closer interest in the destiny of men than others. See also Helmut Prang, "Hölderlins Götter- und Christus-Bild," in *Hölderlin ohne Mythos* (Göttingen: Vandenhoeck & Ruprecht, 1973), 57, and Hölderlin's poem "Bread and Wine."

3. Just how important the worship of Dionysos was to the ancient Greeks emerges powerfully in Nietzsche's *The Birth of Tragedy.* Through the figure of Dionysos Nietzsche constructed an entire metaphysics based on tragedy, originally the collective worship of the god. Long before him, however, Hölderlin had bent his will toward regaining access to the mysteries of Dionysos and in such a way that he fused paganism and Christianity without obliterating either one; on the contrary, in "Bread and Wine," the nature of Christ as a demigod enriches one's perception of Christianity.

4. GSA 2, 1, 48.

5. Ibid., 91. The powers of the night in relation to becoming open, cleared, for the arrival of a deeper, nonrational experience, were perhaps best reflected by the poet Novalis (Friedrich von Hardenberg), whose lyrical work "Hymns to the Night" deserves careful reading in this context.

6. Ibid., 93.

7. Ibid., 94.

8. Ibid., 95. The mingling here of Christian and pagan fulfills a higher aspiration and a higher hope in the poet, for Christ is not seen as the savior. Instead, he is the most recent manifestation of a line of demigods who commune with man, and therefore Hölderlin sees him in the same light as the earlier figures of Greek mythology. Hölderlin was well schooled in Scripture and was intended for the ministry, but the preparation of man for the reception of the divine did not limit itself in him to a particular faith or denomination. It could be argued, if a theological discussion were at stake here, that embracing one religion, as opposed to embracing religiosity per se, is one of the great obstacles to awakening that Hölderlin had to overcome on his own, and that our time must also overcome.

9. One can't help but be reminded of Nietzsche's prophetic writing in the prologue to *Thus Spoke Zarathustra,* where Zarathustra's admonitions fall upon deaf ears, and he exclaims: "Where is the lightning to lick you with its tongue? Where is the madness with which you must be inoculated?" (see *Zarathustra,* prologue no. 3).

10. GSA 2, 1, 94.

11. I see this idea illustrated also in "The Archipelago." Hölderlin renders a history of ancient Greece in this elegiac treatise (296 lines); as the poet entrusted with preserving the memory of the ancients and their gods, he promises (lines 210 ff.) to consecrate the soil of antiquity with his own tears and with water in an act of sacrifice to keep alive the names that threaten to fall into oblivion. Lines 215–19:

There in the silent valley, at the hanging cliffs of Tempe,
I want to live with you, there often, you glorious names!
To summon you by night, and when you appear angrily,
Because the plow desecrates your graves, with my heart's voice
And with pious song I want to atone for you, holy shadows! (GSA 2,1, 109).

12. Eric Santner, *Friedrich Hölderlin: Narrative Vigilance and Poetic Imagination* (New Brunswick: Rutgers U. P. 1986), 92–93.

Chapter 4

1. GSA 2, 1, 99.

2. Ibid. At this point translation of Hölderlin clearly becomes interpretation, because Michael Hamburger renders the final line of the poem this way: "Cares like these in his soul; not, though, the wrong sort of cares" (*Friedrich Hölderlin. Poems and Fragments,* trans. with notes Michael Hamburger (Cambridge: Cambridge U.P., 1980), 261. The German is equivocal on this point, but I favor Martin Heidegger's reading of the lines, which make *die anderen* ("the others") others in a more general sense, not the modifier of "cares" in the penultimate line. Heidegger gives a cogent explanation of the lines in question in *Erläuterungen zu Hölderlins Dichtung* (Frankfurt am Main: Klostermann, 1981), 27–31. For those who do not read German, let this synopsis of the philosopher's reasoning clarify the lines.

The homecoming is an act that involves others, but for which the poet is the catalyst: "The vocation of the poet is the homecoming, through which the homeland is first prepared as the land of nearness to the origin (*zum Ursprung)*" (28). The poet can therefore help reveal the homeland to his relatives, that is, to those related to him whether by blood or not. Heidegger points out that the theme of worry, or care, is voiced early in the poem, in strophe 3, and that the term *the others* figures prominently in the poem "The Poet's Vocation," as we explored the poet's role in joining others in order to be helpful.

3. GSA 2, 1, 92.

4. Ibid., 118.

5. Ibid., 119.

6. Ibid., 92.

7. The reader will find a reflection of this important Hölderlinian theme in the early writings of Nietzsche. During the years of the romantic phase, characterized by the close friendship with Wagner and an obvious respect for Kant, Goethe, Schiller, and Hölderlin, Nietzsche perceived of the Dionysian state as one that required the total suspension of individuality in order for poetry (the lyrical) to speak through the lyrist. The Primal Unity, according to Nietzsche, suspends individuation in the act of poetry, which was also of course Dionysian worship, so that to speak of "lyrical subjectivity" as do the poets of modernity is oxymoronic (see esp. chap. 5). It may be safely assumed that young Nietzsche's writings were indeed informed to some extent by Hölderlin's writings, but, unfortunately, Nietzsche soon tired of his spiritual mentors and literary predecessors, and Hölderlin (with a host of others) was cast into the pit.

8. Erich Heller and Anthony Thorlby, "Idealism and Religious Vision in the Poetry of Hölderlin," 24.

9. Ibid.

Chapter 5

1. GSA 2, 1, 53. I am working with the second, and longer, version of the poem.

2. Ibid.

3. David Constantine's biographical approach to Hölderlin suggests that he "was preoccupied with memory in the years after Bordeaux. . . . And memory even becomes an animating force and fills the poems with something of the immanence that all of Hölderlin's poetry seeks." See his *Hölderlin* (Oxford: Clarendon Press, 1988), 275.

4. GSA 2, 1, 165.

5. *Friedrich Hölderlin. Eduard Mörike. Selected Poems,* trans. with intro. Christopher Middleton (Chicago and London: U. of Chicago P., 1972), 259.

6. Ibid. Santner discusses the "mapping of the progress of Spirit" in his book, 34–35.

7. GSA 2, 1, 171.

8. Ibid., 172.

9. See also Andrzej Warminski, *Readings in Interpretation: Hölderlin, Hegel, Heidegger* (Minneapolis: U. of Minnesota P., 1987), 75. Warminski writes: "If to interpret 'bestehendes' is also to make it understandable to Germans, the task of 'deutscher Gesang' is translation: the suppression of the letter and its preservation in spirit. But in order for translation to be possible, the 'veste Buchstab' cannot be regarded as *too* solid—that is, inseparable from its meaning—or disregarded as accidental: the translation must be simultaneously secondary and original."

10. See Ernst Behler's excellent historical overview in "Deconstruction versus Hermeneutics: Derrida and Gadamer on Text and Interpretation," *Southern Humanities Review* 21 (1987), 205–6.

11. GSA 3, 535.

12. GSA 2, 1, 189. Bellarmin is Hyperion's friend, to whom his letters are written, in Hölderlin's epistolary novel *Hyperion.* When the poet asks specifically about Bellarmin, he could be referring to his friend Sinclair, but he could also be alluding to the fact that the poet, like the sailor, finds himself without company on his voyages. For the nuances of narrative in *Hyperion* see Mark William Roche, *Dynamic Stillness* (Tübingen: Niemeyer, 1987), 64–70.

13. Ibid.

Chapter 6

1. See Adrian Del Caro, "Kingdom of This World: Whitman and Nietzsche Compared," in *Walt Whitman. Here and Now,* ed Joann P. Krieg (Westport, Conn.: Greenwood Press, 1985), 193–215.

2. GSA 1, 1, 260.

3. Ibid.

4. See *The Birth of Tragedy,* chaps. 14 and 15; quite briefly, Nietzsche argued that Socrates' reliance on reason, and his impatience with anything that relied on the instincts, made him into a zealous theoretical optimist unable to appreciate the mysteries of tragedy and its deity, Dionysos. There is a point, Nietzsche argued, at which the rigorous believer in knowledge as virtue must penetrate to the periphery of his knowledge and there either despair or learn that his saving grace is art.

5. GSA 2, 1, 20.

6. Ibid., 62.

7. Ibid., 144.

8. Ibid., 145.

9. Ibid., 37.

10. Lawrence Ryan, "Zur Frage des 'Mythischen' bei Hölderlin" in *Hölderlin ohne Mythos,* 69, 74.

11. Friedrich Schlegel, *Gespräch über die Poesie* in *Kritische Friedrich-Schlegel-Ausgabe,* vol. 2, 312.

12. In particular, one could study "Menons Lament for Diotima" in this light, for the poet, having lost his most beloved, finds solace in his vocation and renewed hope that "speaks in him like a god, animating him." GSA 2, 1, 78. We have already studied "To the Fates" in a different context, but clearly the poet who appeals to the Fates for one more summer and autumn in which his song will ripen is also attesting to poetry as the manifestation of life; if only once the poet succeeds in bringing forth his song, then he will have lived *like the gods* (GSA 1, 1, 241).

13. GSA 1, 1, 305.

Chapter 7

1. Pierre Bertaux, "War Hölderlin Jakobiner?" in *Hölderlin ohne Mythos*, 7–8.

2. Ibid.

3. Wilhelm Dilthey, *Das Erlebnis und die Dichtung. Lessing. Goethe. Novalis. Hölderlin* (Leipzig: Teubner, 1913), 4th ed., 350.

4. See introduction. Hölderlin was not a reformer, no more, in any case, than was Nietzsche. Yet one does not speak of Nietzsche in terms of "resignation" though he, too, produced great works in relative isolation.

5. Richard Sieburth, ed. and trans. *Friedrich Hölderlin. Hymns and Fragments* (Princeton U. P. 1984), 36.

6. GSA 1, 1, 207.

7. Ibid., 299.

8. *Hyperion*, GSA 3, 153. Surely Nietzsche must have read this passage in Hölderlin, for compare Zarathustra's words from the chapter in which he deals with the "inverse cripples" ("On Redemption"):

This is what is horrifying to my eyes, that I find
men in ruins and scattered about as on a battlefield
and butcher field.

And if my gaze flees from the present to the past:
it finds always the same thing: fragments and piles of limbs
and grisly accidents—but no humans! *Zarathustra, 393.*

9. GSA 3, 156

10. GSA 2, 1, 3.

11. Hölderlin's thesis that the divine spirit wanders from land to land, now animating this people, now another, is reflected in the philosophy of Hegel, who, along with Schelling, was a close friend and collaborator in the mid 1790s. Sieburth glosses their collaboration in his book (9–10), and see also Franz Gabriel Nauen, *Revolution, Idealism and Human Freedom: Schelling, Hölderlin and Hegel and the Crisis of Early German Romanticism* (The Hague: Nijhoff, 1971), 4, 21–26, 50–68.

12. GSA 2, 1, 86.

13. Hölderlin also used the metaphor of melting pearls in wine in "Empedocles." Cleopatra was said to have melted pearls in wine in order to win a bet that she could consume ten million sesterces in one meal.

14. Benn has written concerning the intervals of light and dark as follows: "The alternation of divine and godless periods of history appears to him like the alternation of day and night, or summer and winter. . . . The fact that darkness and cold are regularly followed by light and warmth seemed to him the simplest, and therefore surest, guarantee that the wretched political and social condition of Germany, the spiritual torpor of the age, would not be permanent" (*Hölderlin and Pindar*, 93).

15. GSA 2, 1, 96.

16. By way of speculation on this point: Hölderlin's friend Sinclair suggested to the poet's mother that her son was feigning madness in 1805 because Hölderlin had information concerning a group of radicals who intended to assassinate the elector of Württemberg in order to establish a Swabian republic. See Richard Sieburth, 9–10. Of course this doesn't change the fact that Hölderlin never regained his sanity after 1805, though it does suggest, as does his sympathy for the ideals of the Revolution, that he would have welcomed Napoleon. We should also turn our attention to the poem "Buonaparte," for it exalts Napoleon (the entire poem follows):

Holy vessels are the poets,
 Wherein the wine of life, the spirit
  Of heroes is preserved,

But the spirit of this youth
 The quick one, must it not shatter
  The vessel, were it to grasp him?

Hence let the poet leave him untouched, like nature's spirit,
 For with such substance the master becomes a boy.

He cannot live in the poem and there remain,
 He lives and remains in the world. (GSA 1, 1, 239)

17. GSA 2, 1, 149.

18. The eagle was Zeus's messenger, as the mythology tells us how Zeus sent the eagle to earth to fetch Ganymede, cup-bearer to the gods.

19. Charles Taylor, *Hegel and Modern Society*, 2.

20. Heidegger, *Erläuterungen zu Hölderlins Dichtung*, 29.

21. Ibid., 30.

22. This idea is reflected in Gregory Schufreider's "Heidegger's Contribution to a Phenomenology of Culture," *Journal of the British Society for Phenomenology* 17, no. 2 (1986), 166–85. What Schufreider refutes here and elsewhere is the notion that Heidegger's observations on the *polis*, because they were made in university lectures during the 1930s, are in some manner supportive or suggestive of the fascist regime in Germany. I think Hölderlin provided Heidegger with some of the substance of his writings, and certainly with much inspiration; commentators have also suggested that Heidegger's illuminations of Hölderlin, undertaken during the 1930s and 1940s, are suspect as "political." This does not prohibit the commentators from deferring to Heidegger whenever it is found convenient, however, and for my part Heidegger is justified in pursuing the implications of the poet's relation to his people beyond the attention span of his less patient readers.

23. Schufreider, "Heidegger's Contribution to a Phenomenology of Culture."

24. Schufreider is helpful in underscoring the necessity that Hölderlin attaches to the *expression* of what one is, "one" serving here both to designate the individual and the collective, which might become "One." Let us recall how frequently Hölderlin remarks on the silence of his people, and let this observation on the nature of history in Heidegger illuminate Hölderlin's direction, his drift when he "sings" of the fatherland:

If what Heidegger calls 'history' does not occur because we all stand around together in a time simply passing but is an achievement only attained when resolute individuals have uncovered their own being as time and in so doing have found themselves and chosen to act in light of their place with others in a tradition struggling for the sake of truth, then it is always possible that the conditions under which we are capable of letting such history happen will not be met. Of course, on my view of Heidegger's account of the *polis*, they would paradigmatically *not* be met in 'totalitarianism' with its assertion of the priority of the statesman as the cultural manager of all work, since such a 'totalizing' of the political amounts to quite the opposite of the conditions Heidegger lays out for genuine collectivity. Individuals acting "in light of their place with others" is a fair appraisal of Hölderlin's evocation of the communal spirit, and those "resolute individuals" on whom it is encumbent to uncover being are the poets and the poet's listeners, "the others" of "Homecoming" and "The Poet's Vocation."

25. See, for example, the allusions to his fatherland in letters no. 79, 91, 98, 143 in GSA 6, 1.

26. See letter of Böhlendorff in GSA 6, 1, 433, and the editorial notes in 6, 2, 1020.

27. Friedrich Nietzsche, *Die fröhliche Wissenschaft*. In *Werke*, vol. 2, 134.

Chapter 8

1. Novalis, *Heinrich von Ofterdingen*. In *Schriften*, ed. P. Kluckhohn and R. Samuel, 4 vols. (Stuttgart, 1960), vol. 1, 268.

2. Ibid., 287.

3. Ibid., vol. 2, 647, 685.

4. See Ernst Behler and Roman Struc, trans. *Dialogue on Poetry and Literary Aphorisms* of Friedrich Schlegel. Pennsylvania U.P., 1968.

5. One should turn in particular to *Being and Time*, pt. 1, chap. 4, and the discussion of *das man* (the "they"), and the essays in *Poetry, Language, Thought*, trans. Albert Hofstadter (New York: Harper and Row, 1971), 34.

6. Heidegger, *Poetry*, 72, 94.

7. Paul de Man, *Blindness and Insight*, 31.

8. I do not wish to praise Hölderlin at the expense of his contemporaries, but some statement putting his work into perspective must be ventured out of fairness to him and to his peers. There is irony in the fact that Novalis, regarded as one of the period's greatest lyric poets, and certainly a prolific contributor to theoretical romanticism, is frequently cited on the vocation of the poet, inasmuch as most of his poetry and much of his theoretical writing explores the world of the dead (literally here, not only as the world of the past). Yet Hölderlin, one might say quietly but with a genius that would rescue poetry from neurosis, treated the real issue of our own time and place.

9. I am not certain that either Michael Hamburger or Christopher Middleton have rendered this sentence accurately, for both emphasize that "the others" help the poet to understand something, whereas Hölderlin wrote (essentially) "by this they understand helping," meaning either that the others understand helping when the poet turns to them or, more logically, the poets understand what it means to help when they turn to the others. See GSA 2, 1, 48.

10. See Beissner's commentary to these political interpretations, and his own suggestions, in GSA 3, 549, 551.

11. GSA 3, 532.

12. Ibid., 535.

13. Ibid.

14. Ibid., 536.

15. The identity of the prince of the feast is the subject of much controversy, as indicated by Hamburger in his notes (661–2), and Beissner in his detailed notes reviewing the literature on "Celebration of Peace" (GSA 3, 547–68). Beissner comes to a conclusion that is consistent with Hölderlin's conception of the poet as preserver and preparer of a place for the gods; the "prince of the feast" is the personification of man's willingness to experience an imminent, new encounter

with the divine through the figure of a mediator-god, just as Dionysos and Christ represent stages of this readiness in the history of mankind. More on this in the next chapter dealing with H.'s conception of the divine.

16. GSA 2, 1, 188–89.

17. Ibid., 117.

18. Friedrich Nietzsche, *Die fröhliche Wissenschaft.* In *Werke,* Vol. 2, 116. *Gay Science* aphorism no. 109.

19. *Jenseits von Gut und Böse, Werke,* Vol. 2, 689. *Beyond Good and Evil,* no. 225.

20. *Also sprach Zarathustra, Werke,* Vol. 2, 344.

Chapter 9

1. GSA 1, 1, 250.

2. Dilthey, *Das Erlebnis und die Dichtung,* 360.

3. Heller and Thorlby, "Idealism and Religious Vision," 24.

4. GSA 1, 1, 263–64.

5. Ibid., 298.

6. Ibid., 300.

7. GSA 2, 1, 28.

8. GSA 3, 537–58.

9. For this idea I am indebted to Gregory Schufreider, who worked out the equation in a manuscript on Heidegger, using Heidegger's reading of Hölderlin to illuminate the question of the divine in Heidegger.

10. GSA 1, 1, 274.

11. GSA 2, 1, 3–5.

12. Ibid., 77.

13. Ibid., 78.

14. Ibid., 91.

15. Ibid.

16. End of strophe 3, 91.

17. GSA 2, 1, 37.

18. Ibid., 152.

19. Ibid., 145.

20. Ibid., 147.

21. See Richard Sieburth, 117–18 and 268. I will use Sieburth's version, based on Sattler's *Frankfurter Ausgabe,* as the two remaining strophes are the same in Beissner. Heidegger used the same version, or one very near to it, in his essay "What are Poets For?" ("Wozu Dichter?") in *Poetry, Language, Thought,* 91–142.

22. GSA 2, 1, 195–96.

23. Sieburth, *Friedrich Hölderlin. Hymns and Fragments,* 23.

24. GSA 2, 1, 189.

25. Stanley Corngold, *The Fate of the Self: German Writers and French Theory* (New York: Columbia U. P., 1986), 36.

26. GSA 2, 1, 195. I prefer Beissner's reading of this line (2, 2, 825), with "es tönet das Blatt" as the music of the poetic word, over Sieburth's reading: "The rustle of leaf and then the sway of oaks / Beside glaciers" (117).

27. GSA 2, 1, 91.

28. These strophes are of the third version of the poem, which both Sieburth and Hamburger follow. GSA 2, 1, 197–98.

29. See Beissner's notes to "Mnemosyne" 2, 2, 824–30.

30. GSA 2, 2, 827–28.

31. Beissner, GSA 2, 2, 829.

Chapter 10

1. GSA 2, 1, 91.

2. See also my discussion of this theme in "Nonmetaphysical divinity?"

3. Friedrich Nietzsche, *Sämtliche Werke. Kritische Studienasugabe in 15 Bänden,* ed. Giorgio Colli and Mazzino Montinari (Berlin: de Gruyter, 1980), vol. 11, 257. (Henceforth as KSA followed by vol. and page.)

4. Heidegger, *Hölderlins Hymne "Andenken"* (Frankfurt: Klostermann, 1982), 78.

5. Schlegel, *Athenäum,* vol. 2, 189.

6. Nietzsche, *Werke,* vol. 1, 222.

7. No. 289, *Werke,* vol. 1, 1038.

8. *Werke,* vol. 3, 1371.

9. No. 289, *Werke,* vol. 2, 168.

10. *Werke,* vol. 2, 161.

11. *Ecce homo, Werke,* vol. 2, 1124.

12. Ibid.

13. *Briefe, Werke,* vol. 3, 1215.

14. KSA 10, 588.

15. *Werke,* vol. 2, 405.

16. Ibid.

17. Ibid.

18. See Adrian Del Caro, "The Immolation of Zarathustra: A Look at the Fire Beacon," *Colloquia Germanica* 17:3/4 (1984), 251–56.

19. *Werke,* vol. 2, 480.

20. KSA 11, 581–83.

21. After he had decided that his own efforts to reclaim the portal to antiquity far surpassed those of his predecessors, Nietzsche denied that thinkers such as Winckelmann and Goethe had discovered this entry. See KSA 11, 424.

22. *The Gay Science, Werke,* vol. 2, 271.

23. KSA 10, 108.

24. Ibid. 11, 328.

25. KSA 10, 12; *Gay Science, Werke,* vol. 2, 271; KSA 10, 34; KSA 10, 108; KSA 10, 53; KSA 11, 328; and the Naumann edition of 1906, vol. 8, 356.

26. GSA 6, 1, 47.

27. Ibid., 87.

28. Ibid., 232.

29. Ibid., 235–37.

30. His affair with Susette Gontard, the banker's wife, apparently became known, and Hölderlin was eventually forced to resign, whereupon he fled to Homburg in order to remain close to her in Frankfurt.

31. GSA 6, 1, 263.

32. Beissner writes that Hölderlin had begun a Columbus poem as early as 1789, while Sieburth claims the poem was first drafted in 1801, later elaborated in 1805 and 1806. See GSA 2, 2, 880, and Richard Sieburth, *Friedrich Hölderlin. Hymns and Fragments* (Princeton, 1984), 275.

33. GSA 2, 1, 19.
34. Ibid., 105.
35. Heidegger, *Hölderlins Hymne "Andenken,"* 175–76.
36. GSA 2, 1, 105.
37. Ibid., 188.
38. *Zarathustra, Werke,* vol. 2, 480.
39. See Sieburth, *Friedrich Hölderlin. Hymns and Fragments,* 184–93, 275–77.
40. Heidegger, 179.
41. Sieburth, 275–77. This shifting of perspective is also found in Nietzsche's Columbus poem.
42. Sieburth, 188.
43. Ibid., 190.
44. Ibid.
45. GSA 2, 2, 880.

Epilogue

1. Bloom, *Deconstruction and Criticism,* 3.
2. GSA 6, 2, 889.
3. Nietzsche, "On the Way of the Creator," *Thus Spoke Zarathustra,* vol. 2, 326.
4. Charles Taylor, *Hegel,* 6.
5. GSA 6, 1, 27.
6. Ibid., 91. Hölderlin had already been practicing for his theological profession by preaching in the villages before he took the final examinations (see letter to Neuffer, October 1793, 95); and in November of 1795, after his first tutorship in the von Kalb household had come to an end, he voiced his anxiety at once again receiving an assignment from the consistory (letter to Ebel, 183). In the same letter he spoke of how the theologists of Würtemberg were too dependent on the consistory.
7. GSA 6, 1, 51, 66.
8. Ibid., 68.
9. Ibid., 169.
10. Ibid., 235, 244.
11. Ibid., 254.
12. Ibid., 264.
13. Ibid., 289, 312.
14. Taylor, *Hegel,* 8, 13.
15. GSA 6, 1, 379.
16. Ibid., 254.
17. Lawrence Ryan, *Hölderlins "Hyperion." Exzentrische Bahn und Dichterberuf* (Stuttgart: Metzlerische Verlagsbuchhandlung, 1965), 233.
18. GSA 6, 1, 261.
19. Taylor, *Hegel,* 4.

Bibliography

Behler Ernst. "Deconstruction versus Hermeneutics: Derrida and Gadamer on Text and Interpretation." *Southern Humanities Review* 21 (1987), 201–23.

Behler, Ernst, and Roman Struc, trans. *Dialogue on Poetry and Literary Aphorisms.* By Friedrich Schlegel. University Park: Pennsylvania U. P., 1968.

Benn, M. B. *Hölderlin and Pindar.* The Hague: Mouton, 1962.

Bertaux, Pierre. "War Hölderlin Jakobiner?" In *Hölderlin ohne Mythos.* Ed. Ingrid Riedel. Göttingen: Vandenhoeck & Ruprecht, 1973, 7–17.

Bloom, Harold. *Deconstruction and Criticism.* New York: Seabury Press, 1979.

Constantine, David. *Hölderlin.* Oxford: Clarendon Press, 1988.

Corngold, Stanley. *The Fate of the Self: German Writers and French Theory.* New York: Columbia U. P., 1986.

Del Caro, Adrian. "Kingdom of This World: Whitman and Nietzsche Compared." In *Walt Whitman Here and Now.* Ed. Joann P. Krieg. Westport, Conn.: Greenwood Press, 1985, 193–215.

―――. *Nietzsche contra Nietzsche: Creativity and the Anti-Romantic.* Baton Rouge: Louisiana State U. P., 1989.

―――. "Reception and Impact: The First Decade of Nietzsche in Germany." *Orbis Litterarum* 37 (1982), 32–46.

―――. "Ethical Aesthetic: Schiller and Nietzsche as Critics of the Eighteenth Century." *Germanic Review* 55 (1980), 55–63.

―――. "The Immolation of Zarathustra. A Look at the Fire Beacon." *Colloquia Germanica* 17 (1984), 16–19.

de Man, Paul. *Blindness and Insight.* New York: Oxford U. P., 1971.

Dilthey, Wilhelm. *Das Erlebnis und die Dichtung. Lessing. Goethe. Novalis. Hölderlin.* 4th ed. Leipzig: Teubner, 1913.

Guthrie, W. K. C. *A History of Greek Philosophy.* Cambridge: Cambridge U. P., 1965, vol. 2.

Hamburger, Michael, trans. *Friedrich Hölderlin. Poems and Fragments.* Cambridge: Cambridge U. P., 1980.

―――. *Hölderlin.* 2d ed. London: The Harvill Press, 1952.

Hardenberg, Friedrich von. [Novalis] *Heinrich von Ofterdingen.* In *Novalis Schriften.* Ed. Paul Kluckhohn and Richard Samuel. Stuttgart: Kohlhammer, 1960, vols. 1–2.

137

138 BIBLIOGRAPHY

Heidegger, Martin. *Erläuterungen zu Hölderlins Dichtung.* Frankfurt am Main: Klostermann, 1981.

———. *Hölderlins Hymne "Andenken."* Frankfurt am Main: Klostermann, 1982.

———. *Poetry, Language, Thought.* Trans. Albert Hofstadter. New York: Harper and Row, 1971.

Heller, Erich, and Anthony Thorlby. "Idealism and Religious Vision in the Poetry of Hölderlin." *Quarterly Review of Literature* 10: 1 and 2 (1959), 23–40.

Hölderlin, Friedrich. *Hölderlin: Sämtliche Werke.* Ed. Friedrich Beissner. 8 vols. Stuttgart: Cottasche Buchhandlung, 1946–85.

———. *Briefe.*

———. *Gedichte bis 1800.*

———. *Gedichte nach 1800.*

———. *Hyperion.*

Kuzniar, Alice. *Delayed Endings: Nonclosure in Novalis and Hölderlin.* Athens, Ga.: U. of Georgia P., 1987.

Middleton, Christopher, ed. and trans. *Friedrich Hölderlin. Eduard Mörike. Selected Poems.* Chicago: U. of Chicago P., 1972.

Mieth, Günther, ed. *Friedrich Hölderlin Werke in zwei Bänden.* Stuttgart: Parkland, 1970, vol 1.

Nauen, Gabriel. *Revolution, Idealism and Human Freedom: Schelling, Hölderlin and Hegel and the Crisis of Early German Idealism.* The Hague: Nijhoff, 1971.

Nietzsche, Friedrich. *Werke in drei Bänden.* Ed. Karl Schlechta. Munich: Hanser, 1966.

———. *Also sprach Zarathustra.*

———. *Aus dem Nachlaß der 80er Jahre.*

———. *Briefe.*

———. *Die fröhliche Wissenschaft.*

———. *Ecce homo.*

———. *Jenseits von Gut und Böse.*

———. *Morgenröte.*

———. "Vom Nutzen und Nachteil der Historie für das Leben."

———. *Kritische Studienausgabe.* Ed. Giorgio Colli and Mazzino Montinari. Berlin: de Gruyter, 1980, vols. 10–11.

Prang, Helmut. "Hölderlins Götter- und Christus-Bild." In *Hölderlin ohne Mythos,* 48–67.

Roche, Mark William. *Dynamic Stillness: Philosophical Conceptions of "Ruhe" in Schiller, Hölderlin, Büchner, and Heine.* Tübingen: Niemeyer, 1987.

Ryan, Lawrence. *Hölderlins "Hyperion". Exzentrische Bahn und Dichterberuf.* Stuttgart: Metzlerische Verlagsbuchhandlung, 1965.

———. "Zur Frage des 'Mythischen' bei Hölderlin." In *Hölderlin ohne Mythos,* 68–90.

Santner, Eric. *Friedrich Hölderlin: Narrative Vigilance and Poetic Imagination.* New Brunswick: Rutgers U. P., 1986.

Schiller, Friedrich. *Über die aesthetische Erziehung des Menschen in einer Reihe von Briefen.* In *Schillers Werke in zwei Bänden.* Ed. Erwin Ackerknecht. Munich: Droemersche Verlagsanstalt, 1954), vol. 2.

Schlegel, Friedrich. *Kritische Friedrich-Schlegel-Ausgabe.* Ed. Hans Eichner and Ernst Behler. Munich: Schöningh, 1967, vol 2.

———. *Gespräch über die Poesie.*

———. *Kritische Fragmente.*

Schufreider, Gregory. "Heidegger's Contribution to a Phenomenology of Culture." *Journal of the British Society for Phenomenology* 17:2 (1986), 166–85.

Sieburth, Richard, trans. and intro. *Friedrich Hölderlin. Hymns and Fragments*. Princeton: Princeton U. P., 1984.

Taylor, Charles. *Hegel and Modern Society*. Cambridge: Cambridge U. P., 1979.

Unger, Richard. *Friedrich Hölderlin*. Boston: Twayne Publishers, 1984.

Warminski, Andrzej. *Readings in Interpretation: Hölderlin, Hegel, and Heidegger*. Minneapolis: U. of Minnesota P., 1987.

Index of Poems Cited

141

Index